VOGUE GUIDE TO NEEDLEPOINT Tapestry

COLLINS: LONDON AND GLASGOW

IN ASSOCIATION WITH THE CONDÉ NAST PUBLICATIONS LTD

First published 1974

Published by COLLINS—LONDON & GLASGOW
in association with THE CONDÉ NAST PUBLICATIONS LTD
COPYRIGHT © 1974 THE CONDÉ NAST PUBLICATIONS LTD

ISBN 0 00 435055 3

Filmset by Typesetting Services Limited, Glasgow
Printed in Great Britain. Collins Clear-Type Press

Editor: Judy Brittain
Assistant Editor: Rosemary Lamont
Designs: Susan Mann MA, RCA
Editor Condé Nast Books: Alex Kroll

Contents

Acknowledgements:

Drawings: Barbara Firth – pages 9–37, 48–49. Susan Mann – pages 40–47, 50–77. Photographs: Olivero Toscani – front cover and page 62. John Swannell – back cover and page 78. John Wingrove – front end paper. Alessandro Magris – back end paper. Maurice Dunphy – pages 4, 10–37 and back cover. David Mann – page 76

All colours given are for Coats Anchor Tapisserie wool unless otherwise stated

4

Introduction

Needlepoint tapestry or canvas work embroidery, is an easy, useful and interesting craft. It dates back to the Middle Ages when it was used to copy the beautiful woven tapestries which only the rich could afford. These 'copy' tapestries were so hard-wearing that, whereas the originals have long since perished, the 'copies' still exist and, in fact, are the only record of the previous work.

Needlepoint tapestry can either be very quick or very slow to do. The speed depends entirely on the gauge of canvas being used and the amount of detail in the work. For instance an intricate Petit Point design will take a great deal longer than a rug on a wide mesh canvas with thick wool. The famous 'Florentine' work which is often used for chair upholstery, is quick to work and exciting to do for the design grows with each stitch. The choice of colours for 'Florentine' work is also exciting and interesting for the more tones upon tones are used the more fascinating and elaborate the design will become.

When this book has been read and the stitch samples worked, the reader should be ready to take on any needlepoint work. There are many ready-designed canvases available to work with but sometimes these may not be in the exact style or colouring required. The colouring could be altered, but the actual style would be a little difficult to change. Therefore it is hoped that the reader may try designing, as well as working, in needlepoint, because, apart from teaching the various techniques of needlepoint tapestry, the book aims at opening up and expanding the reader's imagination so that designing will come as the next natural move.

Once the designing mind is awakened there will be no limit to the ideas which will come flooding through and onto the canvas via the needle. Anything from sea shells to tiles, and from butterflies to plate patterns can be incorporated into a design. Once this happens the designer is a painter using yarn and a needle instead of paints and a brush.

Mosaic china plate with portrait of Edward VII and a needlepoint copy by Kaffe Fassett

Ingredients

Basically, all that is required is canvas, a needle and a selection of different coloured yarns. If you are going to work out your own design, you will also need a thick nib pen or fine paint brush, India ink, tracing paper and/or graph paper.

On the opposite page are a selection of the various canvases and yarns generally available. The canvases are gauged by threads per inch for the single thread and holes per inch for the double thread. The sizes range from 24 threads to the inch for a really fine work to 10 holes to 3 inches for rugs and thick carpets. The single thread canvas is sometimes known as plain canvas or congress canvas and can be used for nearly everything except trammed work (see page 9). It is better for really fine Tent stitch work than double canvas.

The double thread canvas, sometimes known as Penelope canvas, can be converted into single canvas by working between the threads. This is particularly useful when a fine effect is needed to contrast whilst still using the same stitch. Tent stitch used in this way is known as Petit Point and Tent stitch used on a trammed canvas using the whole mesh is known as Gros Point.

Although these two canvases look different the method of working stitches is exactly the same for either one except when a double thread canvas is particularly mentioned and then the stitch being used may be incorporating work between the threads.

The needles for tapestry come in the various sizes shown. The points are rounded in order to avoid splitting yarn or breaking canvas threads. The eyes are long and slim so as not to distort the holes when stitches are being worked. The yarns which can be used for tapestry are numerous, from silks and wools to synthetics and raffia, anything, in fact, which will cover the canvas. The most usual yarn is wool and tapestry wools come in a very wide range of colours. The quantity of yarn needed will vary according to the stitch and canvas being used but as a rough guide 1 oz will cover 24″ × 2″ in Gros Point. The finer the canvas the finer the yarn. The crewel wool is ideal for Petit Point. Strands of it can also be used in conjunction with tapestry wool to enhance a colour effect or to bulk out the tapestry wool a little in order to fill the canvas. The stranded silk is used for fine work, separating the strands according to the gauge of the canvas. It is also used to highlight areas of a design. The cotton yarn is used in exactly the same way as tapestry wool. It is particularly successful in Upright Gobelin stitch (page 13). The Turkey wool and Sudan wool are for the wide gauge canvases which are used for rug and carpet work. When choosing colours it is best to seek professional advice about the exact amount needed for a specific colour, because it is advisable to buy the complete amount at one time from the same dye lot. These dye lots do vary in colour and quite a patchy result can be caused by not using the same one throughout.

Frames are not absolutely necessary especially if only a small piece is being worked and is being done in straight stitches following the warp (vertical threads) and weft (horizontal threads) of the canvas. If the work is more complicated, then it may become crumpled without a frame. There are many different types of frame available but for immediate and economical use a picture frame will work well. The canvas should be tin-tacked firmly to the frame. The frame can then be supported on the edge of a table with the lower side on the worker's knees or resting on the arms of the worker's chair.

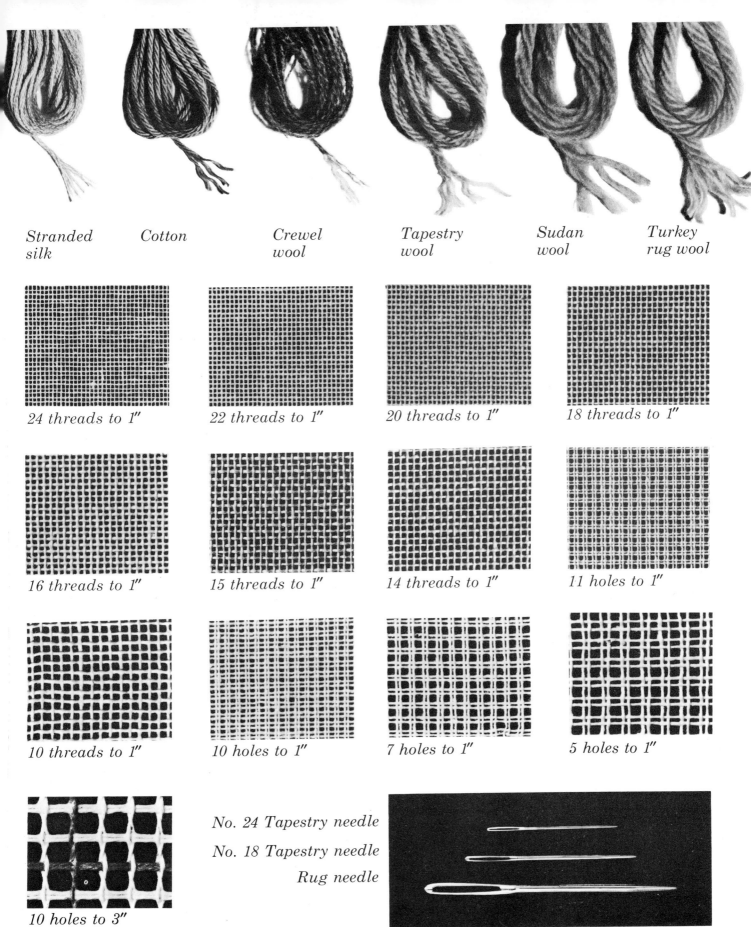

Stranded silk Cotton Crewel wool Tapestry wool Sudan wool Turkey rug wool

24 threads to 1"

22 threads to 1"

20 threads to 1"

18 threads to 1"

16 threads to 1"

15 threads to 1"

14 threads to 1"

11 holes to 1"

10 threads to 1"

10 holes to 1"

7 holes to 1"

5 holes to 1"

10 holes to 3"

No. 24 Tapestry needle

No. 18 Tapestry needle

Rug needle

7

How to start

The easiest way to start to learn how to do needlepoint tapestry is to make a sampler of some of the many stitches. This sampler need not be thrown away later but should be made as beautiful as possible. Therefore the colours should be carefully selected and the correct canvas chosen. The finer the work the smaller the mesh of the canvas and vice versa.

Prepare the canvas first by cutting it to the size required leaving an extra 2″ of unworked area all round. The unworked area is very important, as this is where the canvas will be secured for stretching later. Therefore, if a 12″ square cushion is being made, a 14″ square area of canvas needs to be cut. Secure the edges of canvas with sticky tape or turn over and tack. This is to prevent the canvas from fraying, which is not only maddening but also can become so bad that the 2″ area disappears completely and the frayed ends of the canvas become very involved with the stitches being made. If a sampler is going to be made, then work out the space required for each stitch. The easiest method, of course, is to divide the canvas into 12 equal squares. Delineate these squares (and the design) in India ink. When ink is dry and colours worked out stitching can begin. Start, not by knotting the yarn, but by holding about 1″ of the end at the back of work and secure this end by working over it with the next few stitches. Likewise, when finishing do not make a knot into the previous stitch but slot the yarn under the stitches at the back of the work. In this way the back of work will look as neat as the front, and it will also avoid bumps in finished work. It is important to avoid starting and ending in the same places as this causes ridges.

It is best to work with a fairly short length of yarn, about 12″ to 16″, as this avoids it wearing thin with constant friction against canvas. Also, oddly enough, it is quicker to work with a short yarn as it does not have time to become twisted nor the length to get knotted up with itself.

The finished stitches should be regular, even and unsplit. They should be neither too loose nor too tight. A natural tension will develop as the work becomes familiar to the hands. Do not worry if stitches are not completely even to start with, but, if they are very lumpy and irregular or too tight, unstitch and do them again.

Trammed stitches
Should one want to buy an already designed canvas, one of the first questions which will be asked by the shop is whether a trammed or untrammed canvas is wanted. This will mean

nothing to the novice at needlepoint tapestry and may lead to confusion. Tramming is a method of stitching used to back Tent stitch in order to bulk the tapestry and give it a much more hard wearing and longer life. It is principally used for all forms of upholstery and carpeting. Tramming needs to be done on a double canvas and when a painted design is bought which has been already trammed, the tramming is worked in the various colours of the design. There are various methods of doing tramming:

1. For single stitch tramming where the area is not wider than 6″, work running stitches across the canvas bringing the needle through back to front between the small square of the double threads.

2. When working large areas of tramming, for a carpet or rug, then use the split stitch method which starts off in exactly the same way as single stitch and continues the same except the stitches can be made much bigger, up to 5″, and after the first stitch is made the second stitch is worked into it by splitting the yarn. See diagrams.

3. Vertical tramming is sometimes needed to outline areas. The method is the same as above except that it is worked vertically from top to bottom down the narrow pairs of threads and making the next stitch in the following horizontal intersection of canvas.

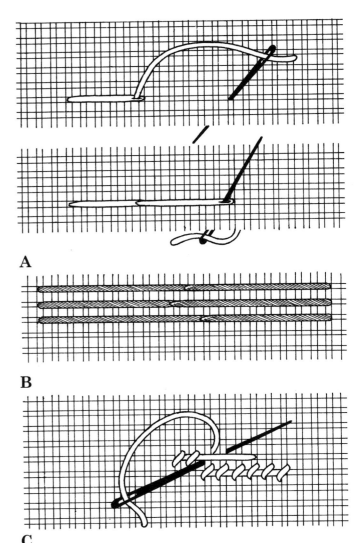

A

B

C

9

10

Stitch samples

Although most of the stitches on the following pages are shown in alphabetical order, Tent stitch, Half Cross stitch, Cross stitch, Upright Gobelin and Wide Gobelin break this rule. The reason being that these five stitches are the basis of all needlepoint tapestry and once mastered the rest should easily follow.

The stitch samples illustrated are mostly in one colour, or, in some cases, two colours. This has been done for clarity but they can be worked in multi-colours, stripes, checks, zig-zags, cubes etc, anything which comes to mind and which will heighten their decorative effect. Once the stitch is mastered, try out some colour sampling.

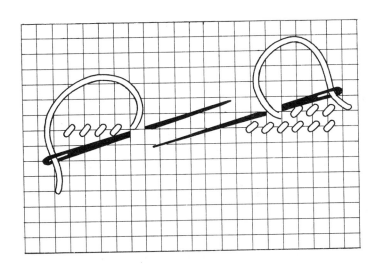

Tent stitch

Work left to right bringing yarn out at top of first stitch; insert needle diagonally down over crossed threads to bottom of the stitch, then bring out to right of first stitch. Continue in this way to end of row. The second row is worked from right to left, inserting the

Sampler cushion in varying shades of blues through to white, worked at the Pearson Gorman Needlepoint School, 164 Campden Hill Road, London W8. The cushion shows many unusual stitches and was made by a complete beginner during a 3-day course.

needle at top of stitch. Continue working rows backwards and forwards until design is complete, making sure that all stitches slope in the same direction. Those on the reverse are longer than those on the correct side. Tent stitch is known as Gros Point when worked on a trammed canvas over the complete mesh and Petit Point when worked between the mesh of double canvas or on a fine canvas. It is very useful for all work, particularly for backgrounds, and in conjunction with other stitches to form delicate lines and outlines.

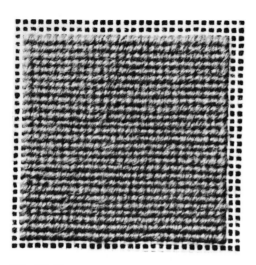

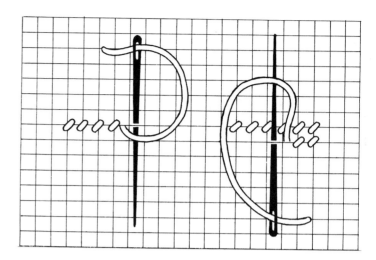

Half Cross stitch or Half stitch

Working left to right from top of canvas, take needle diagonally up across an intersection, insert and bring out one thread below, continue in this way to end of row. To work second row take needle down left over intersection and insert to form new stitch; always inserting needle in vertical position.

Continue in this way row by row. On reverse side stitches will be vertical. This stitch is generally used for backgrounds when yarn is too thick to work a complete Cross stitch. Never use it in conjunction with Tent stitch as this will produce a ridged, amateurish looking surface.

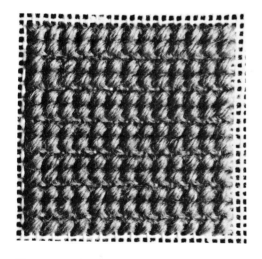

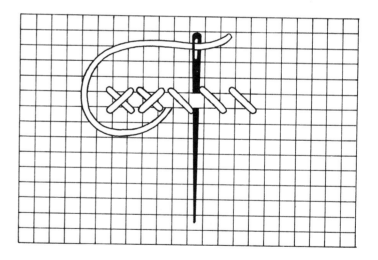

Cross stitch

Working from left to right bring needle out at lower right of first stitch, then insert diagonally up left across 2 intersections and bring it out two threads below, continue this way to end of row. Complete other half of cross as shown. Rows should be worked regularly so that the upper half of all stitches lie in the same direction. The finished cross should form a perfect square and each can be formed individually if interspersed with other stitches. It is an excellent background stitch. For a hard-wearing stitch variation especially good for rugs and carpets, see foot of page 70.

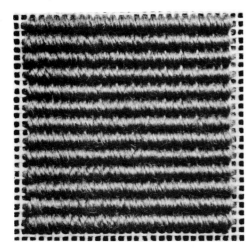

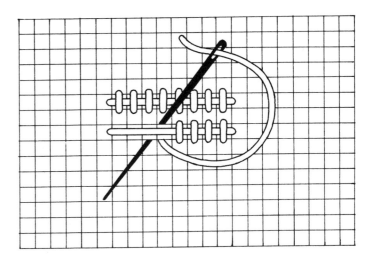

Gobelin stitch, Upright or Straight

This stitch is often trammed to give extra bulk and make it more hard-wearing. Work trammed stitch from left to right, then pull needle through 1 thread down and 1 thread to left, now insert it over 2 threads directly above to form upright stitch, and emerge in position for next stitch 2 threads down and 1 to left. Continue like this, row after row.

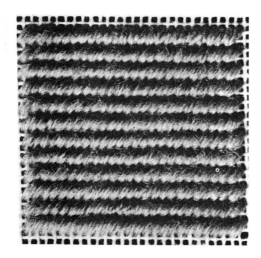

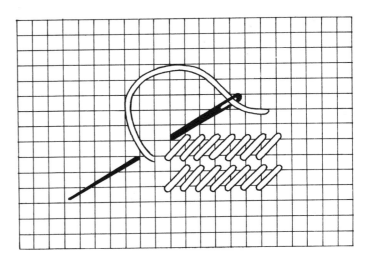

Gobelin stitch, Wide or Oblique

This is also often trammed. The procedure is the same as for Upright or Straight Gobelin but instead of covering the threads with upright stitches they are covered with diagonal or oblique stitches. Pull needle through and up right diagonally across canvas over 2 intersections to form first stitch, insert needle and pull through 1 thread left of base of previous stitch to form next stitch. Continue along this and all following rows in exactly the same way.

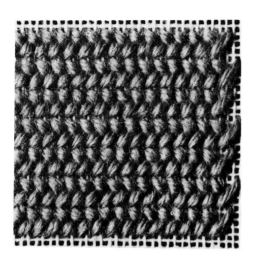

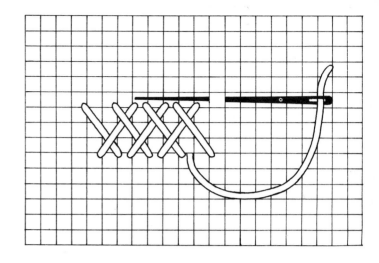

Algerian plaited stitch

Working from left bring needle through and
across 3 threads to the right and 4 down, then
out 2 to the left and up across the first stitch,
3 to the right and 4 up, through and back left
under 2 vertical threads. Continue in this
way as illustrated with next row being
worked directly above previous row.

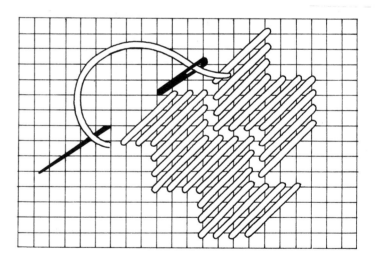

Byzantine stitch

Starting at lower right corner bring needle
through, and up right across 4 intersections,
then through back, 1 thread to left of base.
Work this stitch in regular zig-zag steps.
The illustration shows 4 stitches to each
step, but this could be made smaller or
larger. This stitch is very fast to work.

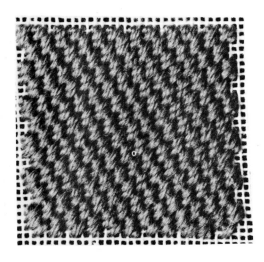

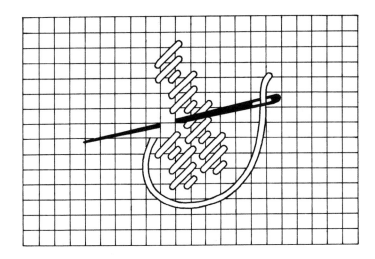

Cashmere stitch

Working from the right, start with a small stitch across one intersection and come out 1 thread to left of base, make second stitch across 2 intersections to form big stitch, make second big stitch above and repeat this sequence of 1 small and 2 big stitches to end of row. Work second row alongside.

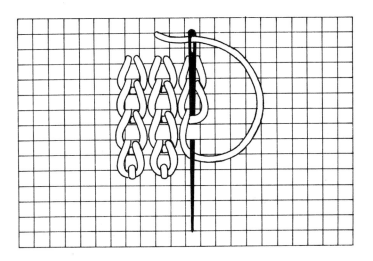

Chain stitch

Work this stitch in vertical rows starting from top left. Bring needle out and hold down yarn with left thumb. Insert needle into same hole and bring it out 2 threads down, drawing through the loop already made, and insert needle into same loop, as illustrated. When using Chain stitch as a filling stitch leave two threads between each row.

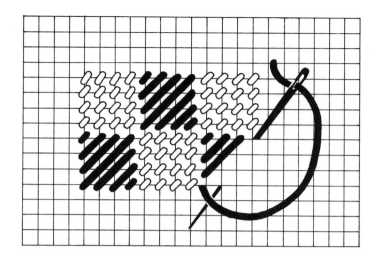

Chequer stitch

Work this stitch over 4 thread squares. Chequer stitch consists of alternating squares of Tent stitch (page 11) and Diagonal stitch (page 21). The best way to work the squares is in diagonal rows beginning at upper left-hand corner. Chequer stitch is used for filling large areas to give a fabric effect, though is equally effective in small areas.

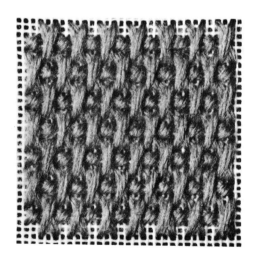

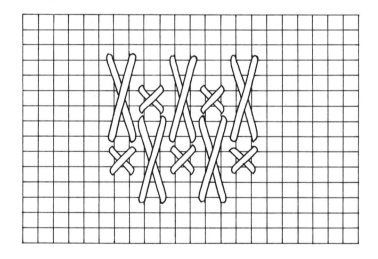

Cross stitch, Alternating or Double stitch

Working from left to right this is a combination of Cross stitch (page 12) and Oblong Cross stitch (page 19). The motifs are worked alternately, small Cross stitch over a 2 thread square and the Oblong Cross over 6 horizontal and 2 vertical threads.

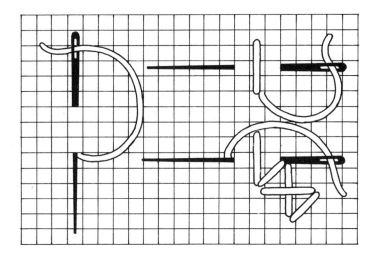

Cross stitch, Diagonal

Work diagonally across canvas from bottom right to top left. This stitch is composed of three small stitches instead of the basic two for Cross stitch. Work upright stitch first, over 4 threads and come out at base, work diagonal stitch up right, across 2 intersections coming out 4 threads to left, work final horizontal stitch of cross as illustrated coming up at same place. Continue in this way across canvas.

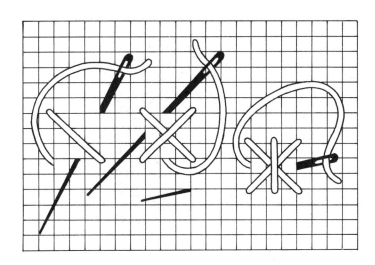

Cross stitch, Double (also known as Leviathan stitch and Smyrna Cross stitch)

Working from right to left, make a basic Cross stitch (page 12) over 4 threads; then bring needle out centre base of cross and make vertical stitch over cross, bring out at centre left and make horizontal stitch, bring out 2 below and 8 to left in readiness for the next stitch, or finish off at the back for one single Double Cross stitch.

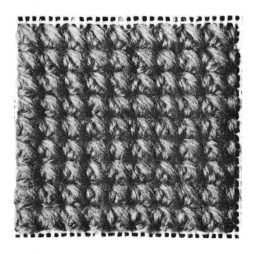

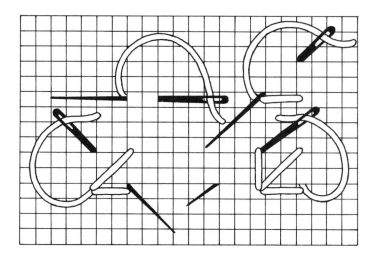

Cross stitch, Italian

Working from right to left, bring needle out and make horizontal stitch right across 3 threads, insert and bring out in exactly the same place, then insert needle diagonally right 3 horizontal threads up from the previous stitch, bring it out again in exactly the same place as before; now insert needle over 3 threads above and bring out diagonally down to the right at the end of first stitch. Finish by working diagonal stitch back across to the head of the upright and bring needle out 3 left of base in position for next stitch.

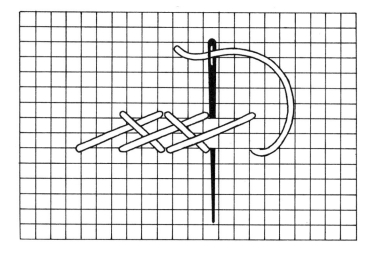

Cross stitch, Long armed

Working from left to right make a long stitch up diagonally right, 3 canvas threads up and 6 across, bring out 3 threads below, then cross diagonally back left over 3 intersections and bring needle out 3 threads below ready for next Long Arm stitch.

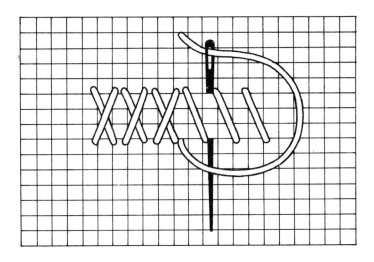

Cross stitch, Oblong

Working from right to left bring needle out at lower right-hand, insert 4 threads up and 2 threads to left, bring out 4 threads below, thus forming a half Oblong Cross stitch, continue in this way to end of row. Work other half of cross as shown. This stitch can be worked from right to left or left to right but it is important, as with all cross stitches that the upper half of all stitches lies in the same direction.

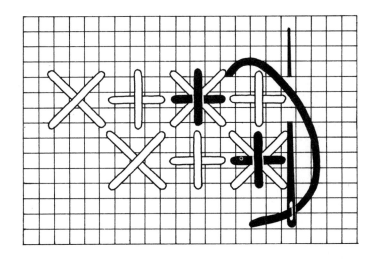

Cross stitch, Reversed

Work this stitch in 2 colours for contrast. Cross stitch reversed is a simple combination of Cross stitch and Upright Cross stitch (page 20) as shown in the illustration. Work alternate stitches of Cross and Upright Cross, then, using contrast colour, work these stitches again but in opposite order so that each completed Reversed Cross stitch is composed of both a Cross stitch and an Upright Cross stitch.

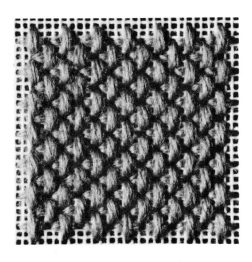

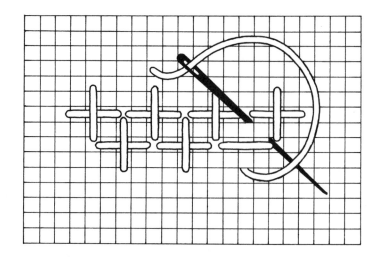

Cross stitch, Upright

Working from left to right bring needle out at left and make a horizontal stitch across 4 threads, bring out 2 threads back and 2 threads down, then work final bar of cross 4 threads above, bringing it out at first insertion, ready for next horizontal stitch.

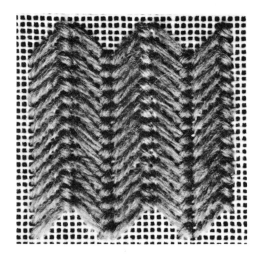

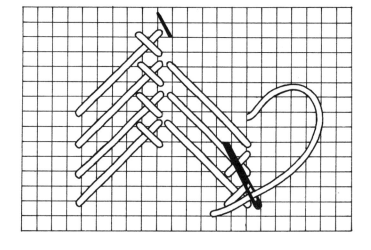

Crossing stitch variation or Fishbone stitch

Worked in 2 separate rows and starting from lower left-hand corner take needle up to the right over 6 intersections, insert needle and bring out 2 threads below, take up to the left over 2 intersections, insert and bring out 2 threads above original base ready for next stitch. Work this row first. Do second row in exactly the same way except that the cross will be formed to the bottom of the long stitch. Continue like this to form Fishbone pattern.

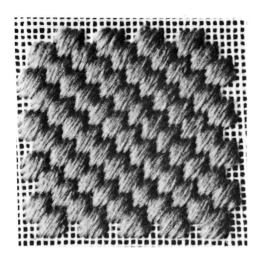

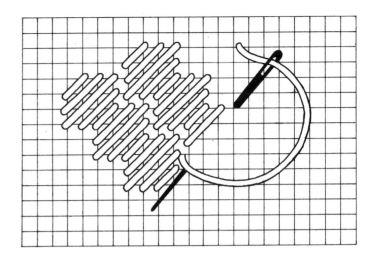

Diagonal stitch

Worked from top left diagonally across canvas. This is an extremely easy and quick stitch to do. The back will look exactly the same as the front. First stitch is made over 2 intersections, second over 3, third over 4, fourth over 3 and fifth over 2, and so on.

Continue like this until row is worked then repeat next row in exactly the same way but making sure that first and shortest stitch is worked diagonally into the same hole as the longest stitch in the previous row so that the two interlock.

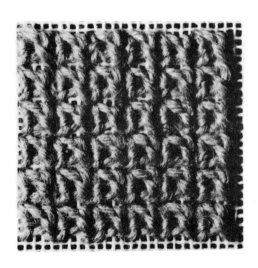

Eastern stitch

Working from left to right, work horizontal stitch across 4 threads, insert needle and bring it out diagonally back 4 threads below beginning, form vertical stitch by inserting needle above at beginning and bring needle out diagonally down 4 threads below first insertion, then take needle under vertical

stitch, over, around and under horizontal stitch, over loop formed and through same hole from which it has just come, bring needle out at first insertion to work next horizontal stitch. Continue in exactly the same way for each row.

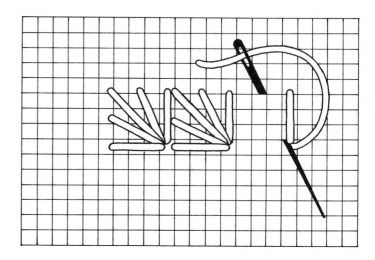

Fan stitch or Ray filling stitch

This is a very simple stitch formed by 5 straight stitches all coming from the same hole and worked to form a square by covering 4 horizontal and 4 vertical threads. Work first upright stitch, then make second stitch 2 threads to the left on the same line, work third stitch in same way, work fourth stitch 2 threads down from third, work fifth horizontal stitch forming square and bring needle 8 threads right to commence next stitch. Continue like this for row. Second row is worked in exactly same way except that Fan stitches point in opposite direction.

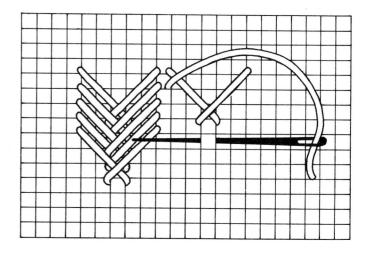

Fern stitch

This is another very simple and effective stitch. Working from top to bottom, left to right, bring needle diagonally down to the right across 4 intersections, insert and bring out 2 threads to left, take up right across 4 intersections, then insert and pull out 1 thread lower than previous stitch in order to commence next. Work next row in exactly the same way forming stitches in same holes at right side of previous row.

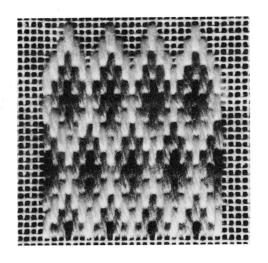

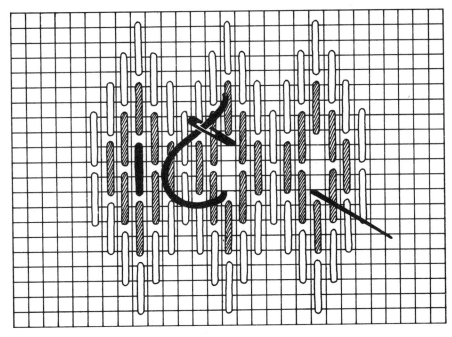

Florentine stitch or Bargello stitch (also known as Cushion stitch, Flame stitch and Irish stitch)

This is an extremely well-known and highly decorative stitch. It is not difficult to do and beautiful colour combinations can be worked. The stitch is used in zig-zags to form a flame pattern. It is generally used to fill big areas and is worked in 2 or more rows of different colours. The size of the zig-zag may vary depending on the number of stitches and threads over which the stitches are worked. It is not advisable to work over more than 6 threads as the stitches are inclined to come loose and catch in things when very large. The stitch is formed by working vertical stitches at thread intervals. The photographed sample is worked over 4 horizontal threads. From left to right work first row making zig-zag 4 stitches high, work second row in second colour and the first stitch of this will be made directly under second stitch of second row and so on (see diagram). The fifth and final row will be in first colour. This completes the diamond pattern photographed and variations of this theme are interesting to work.

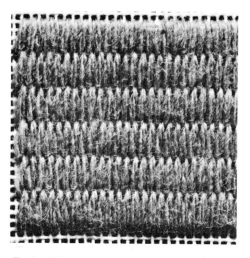

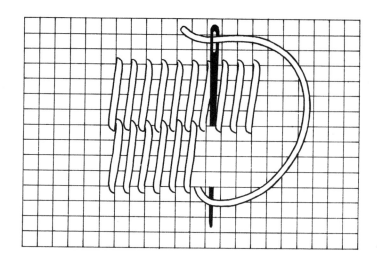

Gobelin encroaching stitch

A very good filling stitch for large areas. Work from left to right over 5 horizontal and 1 vertical thread. The second row is worked 4 threads below the first row and the stitches thus formed will take in the last thread of the previous row and make 'encroaching' stitches. The back of this stitch looks exactly the same as the front.

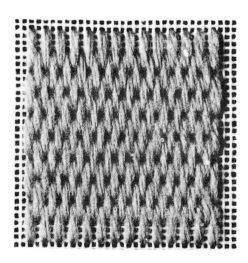

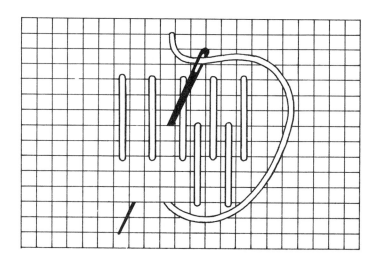

Gobelin filling stitch

A simple stitch to be worked horizontally left to right and right to left. It fills the canvas quickly and when worked in more than one colour is especially suitable for background areas of graduated shading. Upright stitches over 6 horizontal threads are worked into alternate holes with the second row worked 3 threads below the first and overlapping the lower half of the stitches. Subsequent rows are worked into the established pattern.

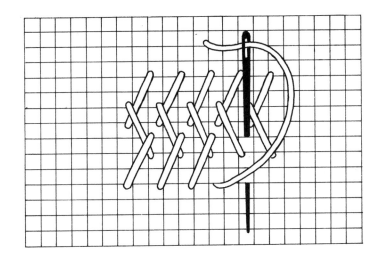

Gobelin plaited stitch

Work from top to bottom and left to right. Make 1 row of diagonal stitches over 4 threads at 2 thread intervals. When row completed work second row of diagonal stitches in opposite direction beginning six threads below last insertion and overlapping as illustrated.

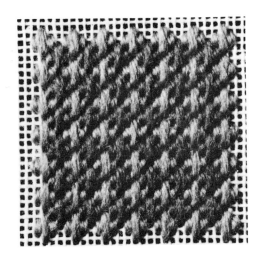

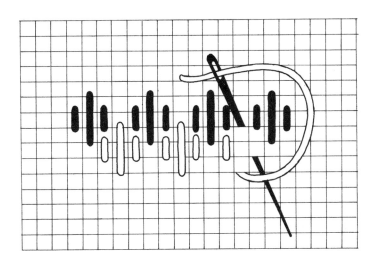

Hungarian stitch

Work in 2 colours from left to right. This is a very simple stitch and is composed of the motif, 1 short stitch, 1 long stitch and 1 short, worked in sequence with a space left between each motif. Work second row in exactly the same way but in contrast colour and with first short stitch coming under third stitch of previous row as illustrated.

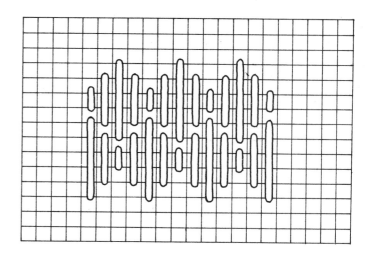

Hungarian stitch variation

This is very like Hungarian stitch except that the sequence of stitches is five instead of three and the two rows interlock. This stitch can be worked in the same or contrast colours. The second row is worked with the longest stitch coming under shortest stitch of previous row.

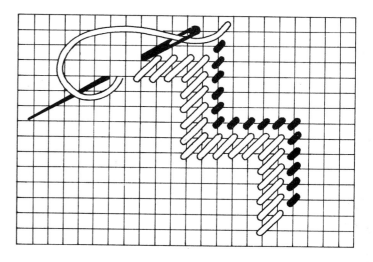

Jacquard stitch

This is a very simple stitch and useful for large areas of background where a patterned or brocaded effect is required. Starting lower right, work 6 diagonal stitches upwards across 2 intersections, then work 5 to left and continue in zig-zag pattern. The second row is worked in contrast colour in Tent stitch and follows the previous row exactly. Continue like this alternating the two stitches.

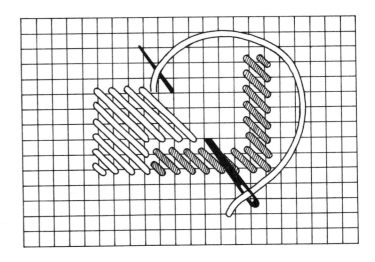

Jacquard stitch variation

This is another background stitch and is quick to work. It can be worked in the same or contrasting colours. Work as shown in diagram with alternate rows of long and short stitches.

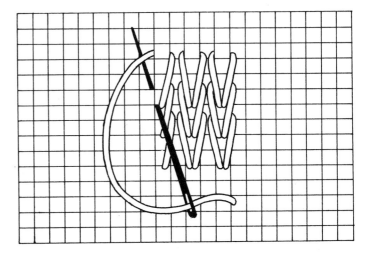

Knitted stitch

This gives exactly the same effect as plain knitting and is therefore particularly useful for realistic, figurative designs. Working from bottom to top and then back again, bring out needle and insert 4 threads up and 1 right, emerge 2 threads down and 1 left ready for next stitch. Continue in this way to end of row, then start to work downwards, bringing out needle 2 to left and inserting at base of previous stitch, thus forming 'knitted look'.

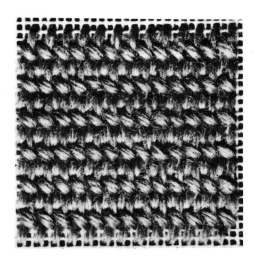

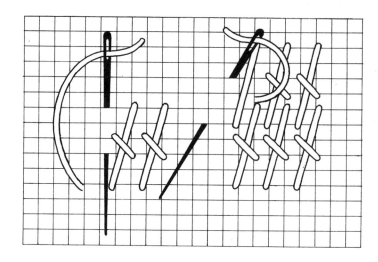

Knotted stitch

Working from bottom make long diagonal stitch 6 threads up and 2 across, insert needle and pull out 4 threads below, then take left across 2 intersections, covering long stitch with a small stitch, insert and pull out 2 threads to left of base ready for next stitch. Following rows are worked in exactly the same way but long stitches are placed between long stitches of previous row.

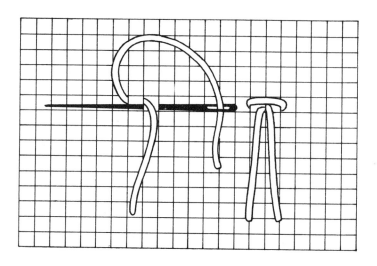

Knotted stitch, Single

This is really a fringe stitch and is useful in figurative design where a fringe is needed. Working from right to left and from front of work pass needle under 2 vertical canvas threads to left leaving end about 1 inch long or as desired, then take needle back over to right and insert 1 vertical thread to right of first insertion, bring needle out 1 thread to left of first insertion, draw stitch up tight and cut thread to same length as first length thus starting to make fringe. Continue like this working stitches close together.

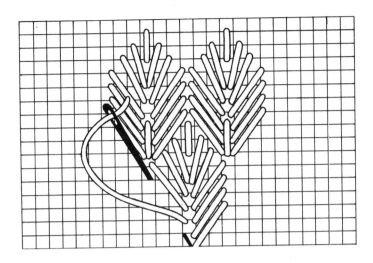

Leaf stitch

Working up canvas on right side of leaf make 4 diagonal stitches above each other over 4 horizontal threads, then make next diagonal stitch 1 thread up and 1 to left over 4 horizontal threads and following stitch in same way, work upright stitch over 3 horizontal threads, forming point of leaf. Work left side of leaf in exactly the same way making another vertical stitch for the stem. Continue to make leaf motifs, leaving no gaps in between each motif.

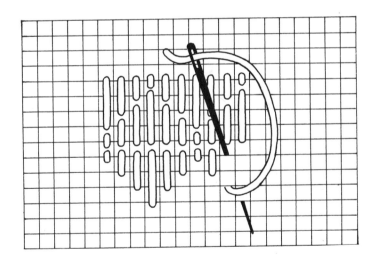

Long stitch or Straight filling stitch

Working from left to right beginning with a long stitch work this pattern exactly as given in illustration making sure that when first 2 pattern rows are completed the third row will be worked into same holes as the bottom of the second row and continue. Four rows make up the completed sequence.

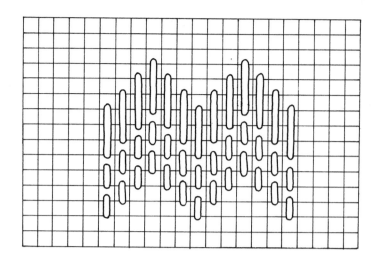

Long stitch variation

Again working from left to right work this pattern row by row as given in illustration. Both this stitch variation and Long stitch are excellent for filling large spaces, being quick to work and interesting to look at.

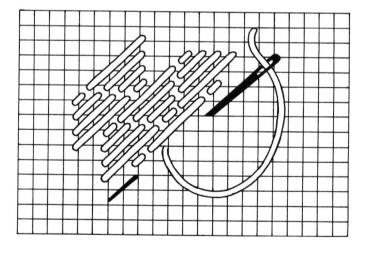

Milanese stitch

A decorative but simple stitch. It gives the appearance of a series of opposed triangles each made up of 4 stitches but the triangles are worked simultaneously across the whole canvas. Start at top left and work diagonally down increasing the length of each row until the centre is reached and from there the rows start to decrease. The first row is worked down the canvas over 4 and 1 intersections, second up over 3 and 2 intersections, third down over 2 and 3 intersections and fourth up over 1 and 4 intersections. These 4 rows form the pattern which is built up with the repetition of the sequence.

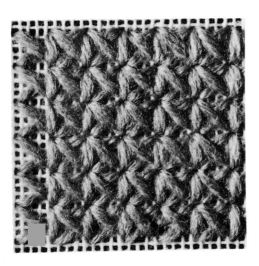

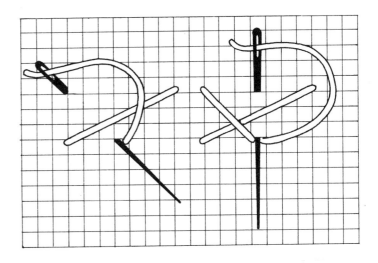

Montenegrin stitch

Working from left to right make diagonal stitch up over 8 vertical and 4 horizontal threads, insert needle and take down 4 intersections to left, emerge and take up over 4 intersections to left, insert and take back to base of the same stitch, emerge and take directly up over 4 horizontal threads, insert and return to base ready for next long diagonal stitch.

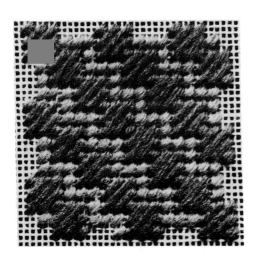

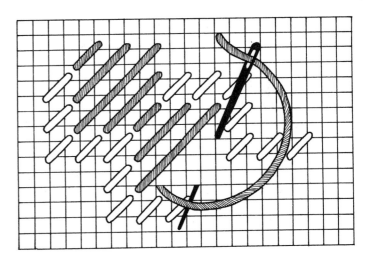

Moorish stitch

Work from left to right diagonally down across canvas in two contrast colours. This stitch is simple to work as shown in illustration. One colour is used for the diagonal stitches over 2 intersections zig-zagged the whole way across the canvas. The second colour is used for the squares built up from 5 graded diagonal stitches.

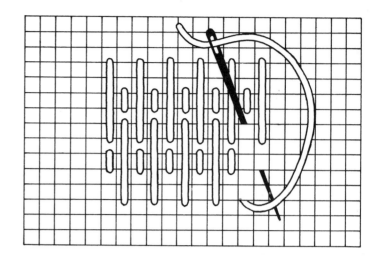

Parisian stitch

This is another good filling stitch and simple to work. Working from left to right first up-right stitch is taken over 6 threads and second over 2 threads, finish row with long stitch. Second row is exactly the same except that it is started and finished with a short stitch.

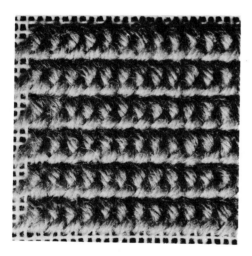

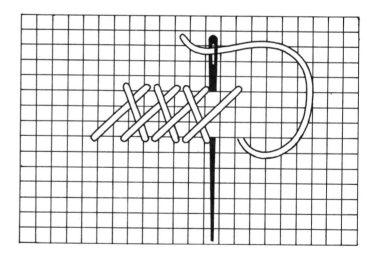

Plait stitch

Worked from left to right across canvas make a diagonal stitch up to right across 4 inter-sections, insert needle and bring out 4 threads below, then cross original stitch, 4 up and 2 to left, insert needle and bring out 4 threads below ready for next stitch. Continue like this for next and following rows always working from left to right and remembering that each row is worked into the bottom of the row before to give close appearance.

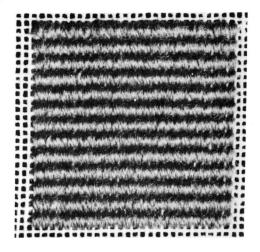

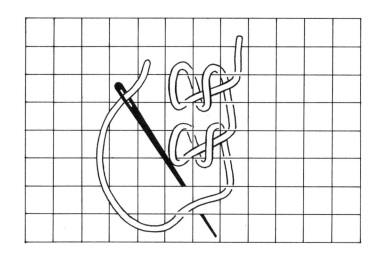

Renaissance stitch

Worked vertically, from top left of canvas this is a very hard-wearing stitch and good for upholstery. Bring needle through and left across 2 vertical threads, insert and bring out immediately below, then take up over 2 horizontal threads, insert and cross diagon- ally under 2 horizontal and 1 vertical thread, pull out and bring up over 2 horizontal threads, insert and bring out 3 horizontal threads down 1 vertical to right ready for next stitch. Continue like this, working each row into right of previous row.

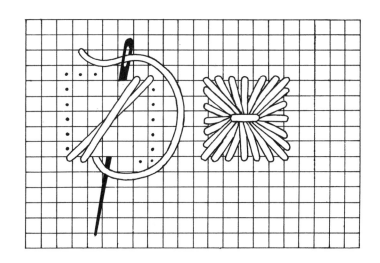

Rhodes stitch

This is a very pretty filling stitch, covering a 6 thread square. Working from left to right, pull needle through and take diagonally up to the right across 6 intersections, insert needle and bring out 6 threads down and 1 thread to right of last stitch, insert up to left of previous insertion and continue like this until square is complete. Finish off with small horizontal stitch at centre, taken through layers of thread and canvas.

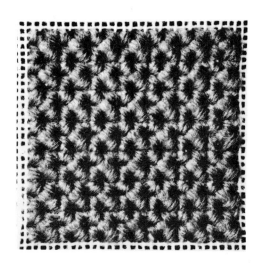

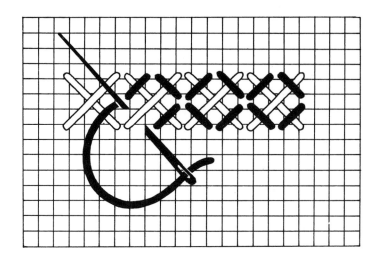

Rice stitch

This is worked in 2 contrasting colours to give greater effect. Even a slight tonal difference between the 2 colours can give a very subtle pattern. The first row is worked in basic Cross stitch over 4 threads. The second row is worked over in diagonal stitches across 2 intersections and worked to form a star between the basic Cross stitch.

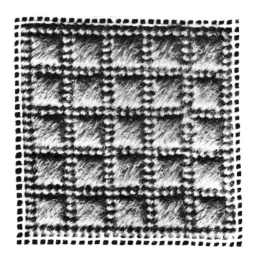

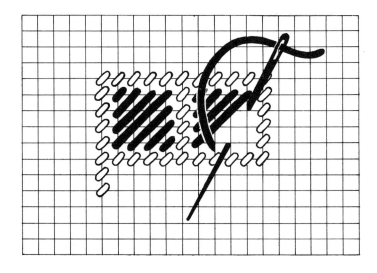

Scottish stitch

Simple and effective stitch worked in 2 colours. More colours could be added to give patchwork effect to squares. Working from left to right, work square of graduated diagonal stitches, first stitch over 1 vertical thread, second over 2, third over 3, fourth over 4, fifth over 3, sixth over 2 and seventh over 1. When square is completed frame it in Tent stitch of contrast colour. Squares can all be worked first and Tent stitch added later as long as space is left.

Shell stitch

This is not a simple stitch and needs to be worked with full attention working from right to left. Make 4 long stitches over 6 horizontal threads, leaving 1 vertical thread between each stitch. When fourth stitch completed bring needle through centre pair of horizontal threads and make a short horizontal stitch right over 1 vertical thread and over the 4 long stitches, drawing them together into a cluster. Continue like this to end of row. When completed link clusters together by coiling contrast thread twice into horizontal stitches. Finish by working back stitches between rows to cover canvas.

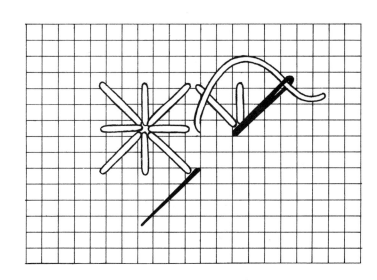

Star stitch

This is a simple stitch worked to form a 6 thread square. The star consists of 8 stitches, each worked from the outside to the centre over 3 threads. Continue from star to star trying to keep back of work the same as front.

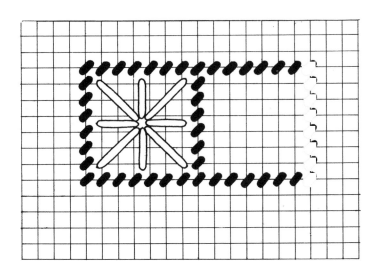

Star on squared background

Work star in exactly the same way as Star stitch but leave gap of 1 vertical and 1 horizontal canvas thread between each star.

When stars completed add Tent stitch in same or contrast colour to frame each star.

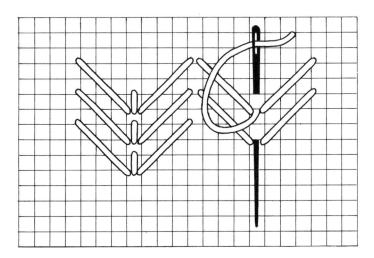

Stem stitch or Herringbone filling stitch

Another simple but effective stitch. Working from top to bottom make a diagonal stitch downwards over 4 intersections, insert needle and bring out 2 horizontal threads below starting point of first stitch. Continue like

this down row. Work second row exactly the same but with diagonals going in opposite direction. When complete work line of back stitch over 2 threads down the middle.

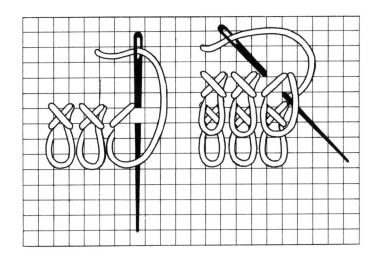

Velvet stitch or Astrachan stitch

This is an interesting stitch which can make very good imitations of Oriental carpets. Working from left to right and from bottom upwards, bring needle out and take up right across 2 intersections, insert needle and bring out again at starting point, re-insert again up right but this time leave loop. To ensure even loops a knitting needle of the required thickness can be used initially to measure each one. Bring needle out 2 horizontal threads below and take up left across 2 intersections to form second part of Cross stitch, insert needle and bring out again down to right, across 2 intersections in readiness for next stitch. After all rows completed cut loops and trim evenly. By working in pattern with this stitch an interesting result can be achieved working with as few as three colours.

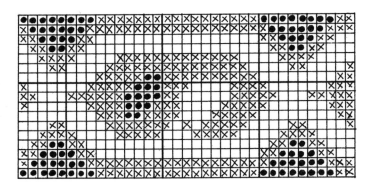

⊠ Prussian blue
⊙ Crimson
☐ Ochre

How to finish, mount and stretch

When the final stitch has been made, run yarn through back of work and finish off. The back of work should be as neat, or nearly as neat, as the front if this method of finishing has been adopted throughout. However, if the back of work is not notable for its neatness it must be tidied up before the final stage of stretching and mounting. Thread through all the odd ends at the back of work, being careful not to put too many in the same place as this will cause a bump or a lumpy surface. Make sure all the canvas is properly covered by stitches. If, by any chance, the yarn has worn thin in a few places, which often happens when it becomes pulled and un-twisted, go over these places with the same colour yarn to fill in. Nothing looks worse than slightly thread-bare work.

Stretching

1. Make an exact cardboard pattern of the finished work; that is, if it is to be a 14″ square cushion, then the pattern should be 14″ square.

2. Lay stitched canvas face down on sheet of plywood or any available and nailable surface and gently wet with sponge or cloth dipped in warm water. Wet lightly and sparingly, unless stitches are very tightly worked or work is mis-shapen, then wet more thoroughly.

3. Fold work in half to ascertain centre front of top and place 1″ nail at this point about $\frac{1}{4}$″ from stitched surface. NB This is why it is important to leave 2″ of unworked canvas all the way round tapestry (see page 8).

4. Lay pattern on top of work and pull opposite side of tapestry to correct length and nail as before.

5. Stretch corners out to pattern and secure each one with nail. (These may have to be adjusted later.)

6. Then pin pattern with light thumb tacks, through centre sides.

7. Stretch out centres of two sides of work and nail as for top and bottom.

8. Place nails $\frac{1}{2}''$ to $1''$ apart all round work making sure that canvas is evenly stretched. Carefully check all corners and adjust nails if necessary. Take time here as it will save trouble later. This is especially necessary if the work is part of a big piece of work where it is vital that patterns match patterns in each piece.

9. Remove pattern.

10. Using a small, stiff $\frac{1}{4}''$ or $\frac{1}{2}''$ brush, work a light layer of wall-paper paste on to back surface and allow to dry. This will take four hours if near heat or two to three days if not. When dry, remove all nails.

The work is now ready to be completed into whatever it is being used for. If a cushion, then trim edges and cut backing of velvet, corduroy or whatever is desired to the same size as tapestry. Sew round three corners making sure that stitches are as close to finished work as possible so that canvas does not show. Insert cushion and either sew up or put in zip so that tapestry may be removed for cleaning from time to time. There are various types of cushion shapes but the example just detailed is the most simple. As a finishing touch, piping cord could be stitched in between the canvas and backing fabric to make it look neat. If the work is part of a big piece, unravel a thread of canvas and use this to stitch each piece together; back stitch making one stitch for every row of canvas; when all pieces are in place trim canvas edges. Then cut layer of carpet felt to exact size of carpet and catch down with upholstery thread. Back this with light canvas, sewing it together inside out on three sides, turning it right side out for fourth side, and

slip stitch together with upholstery thread.

When tapestry has been made to fit a chair, a professional upholsterer should be used to put it in place. It would be sad if so much work had been done and then the final look was somewhat clumsy. On pages 60 and 61 there are ideas and suggestions for chair tapestry.

The only chair which could be entirely done by a non-professional upholsterer is the deck chair, both upright and long. After the work has been stretched and backed simply put it in position and nail it to the wooden supports. The back of work will show on back of chair and therefore an interesting material should be stitched to this to give a good finish. If other types of chairs are being covered and the maker wants to do the entire job, it is advisable to go to evening classes in upholstery so that this craft can be learned thoroughly.

Clothes
The procedure is exactly the same as for cushions, wall-hangings, carpets etc. Great care must be taken to get the finished work stretched to the exact size of the cardboard pattern. The patterns chosen for clothing must be simple and easy to make. Do not choose anything which needs gathering, pleating, tucking or which needs to be darted for shaping. Very plain, simple shapes are best, as it is the tapestry and not the shape which will be the focal point.

Shoes, boots and slippers
Before starting to make any of these items, a pattern shape in the correct size must be obtained from a shoemaker who will be willing to make up the finished work. Otherwise, the procedure is exactly the same, care being taken once more to ensure that the finished work fits the cardboard pattern.

Samples using stitches of same colour

It can be very interesting to work in all one colour and yet achieve a design which is figurative and easily recognizable. One has to think more like a sculptor than a painter when working like this: concentrating on the shape and shadows of the stitches. Aran sweaters, carved ivories, decorative plaster-work, all achieve their effect with just one colour.

The choice of yarns is important—various different yarns may be used all at once in order to get the right highlighting and shading effect. In addition a bead or sequin can be used to pinpoint special highlights.

The stitches should be used so that they will catch light at different angles and throw up or diminish the lines and curves of the design. A double mesh canvas may be more useful for this work as the size of the stitches can be altered.

Design, at left, shows a stitch sampler giving full use to the various stitches used. Overleaf, design of a swan in white and off-whites shows how to achieve amazing results of 'movement' and delicacy with stitches. The black around the head and the orange beak have been used in order to 'hold' the design.

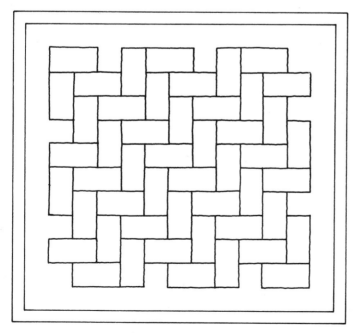

Stitch sampler
Use different stitches to fill each of the 50 rectangles in this interlacing pattern. The size of the design can be varied by altering the number of stitches vertically and horizontally of the rectangle. Use stitches given at the beginning of the book. Work in one colour or tones of a colour. Make up into a cushion or keep as a sampler for reference

Magical monkey tree worked in Gros and Petit Point with blues and greens and high lights of white. Designed and made as a carpet by Angela Fort

40

Samples using stitches of same colour

General note

All colours given are for Coats Anchor Tapisserie wool unless otherwise stated. Areas of blank squares throughout the guide should be filled as indicated around the edge. Any black lines across this area show how stitches should be graduated. In some designs blank squares are part of the key.

Swan

Working design shows a chart to be worked on double canvas using three different Gobelin stitches, Diagonal and Tent stitch

- ■ Black 0403 Trammed Tent stitch
- ⊠ Orange 0315 Trammed Tent stitch
- ⊡ White 0386 Trammed Tent stitch
- ⊡ White 0386 Diagonal stitch
- ▨ White 0386 Wide Gobelin stitch. Work so that complete stitches run along top line of each section
- ⊡ White 0386 Trammed Upright Gobelin
- ◪ Pale grey 0144 Trammed Tent stitch
- ⊡ White 0386 Encroaching Wide Gobelin, trammed, and worked horizontally

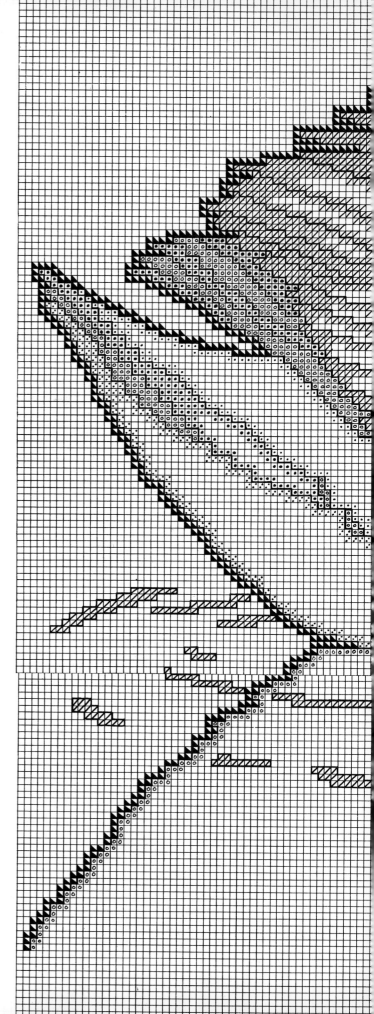

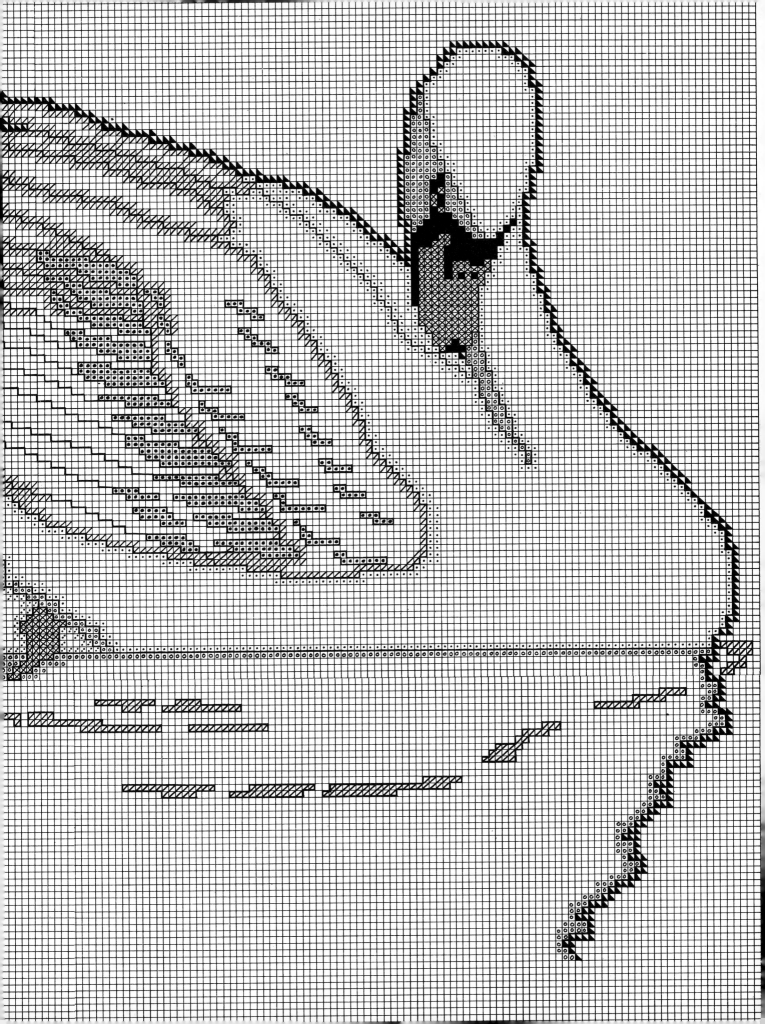

Samples using different colours and yarns

Colour is perhaps the most personal thing about needlepoint tapestry. It is, therefore, with deliberation that colour has not been included in this book, except on the end papers. How to use colour can really only be learnt by observation and experimentation. Observe closely the subtle brown blendings of a moth's wing, the simplicity of a daisy, the variety of colours in a 'blue' Delphinium, the flair and style of an orchid.

Having observed, start to experiment, bearing in mind that in order to achieve results with colour it is important to select several tones of a colour rather than thinking 'I've got a red now let's find a blue'. Fortunately the tapestry wools, silks and cottons come in a huge variety of colours and tones. However, occasionally it is necessary to blend colours together in order to achieve exactly the right tone. For instance one strand of tapestry wool can be used with a strand of crewel yarn or three or four different tones of crewel yarn can be used together in order to get a subtle, marled effect.

Silks, cottons, beads or sequins can also be used to catch the light and capture the effect of, say, a drop of dew on a rose petal. To use different yarns together is perfectly in order as long as they all have the same cleaning requirements. It is therefore best to keep natural fibres with natural fibres and synthetics with synthetics. If beads are used as highlights, they may have to be taken off when the work is being cleaned, and sewn on again later.

Optical effects and perspective illusions are sometimes simply a matter of using different colours in the right position. See working design A. A very good way to learn how to use colour effectively and dramatically is in Florentine or Bargello work, see page 23, for many colours can be used and the sequence of colour can be changed or remain the same according to choice. Working design B shows how results can be achieved. Shading is very important and again close observation of life around you is helpful. Working design C shows a Madonna lily shaded in greens and pinks.

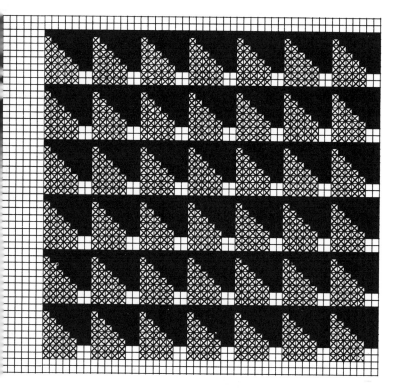

Optical effects sampler (A)
Work in trammed Tent stitch on double canvas.
Repeat pattern to enlarge overall size

■ Dark brown 0360
☒ Rich russet 0501
☐ Background – mid blue 0161

44

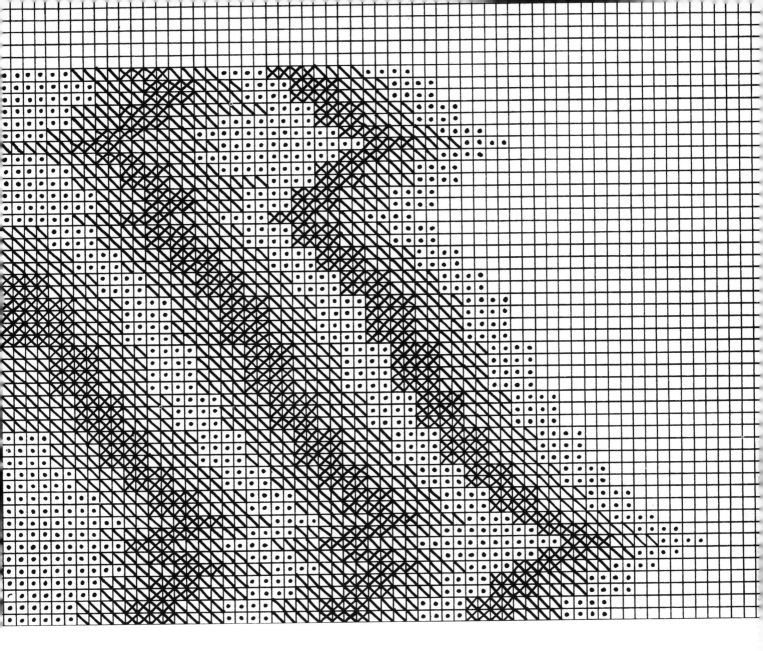

Florentine sampler (B)
*Work in Florentine stitch on single canvas,
making each stitch four squares long*

- ⊡ Pale pastel aquamarine 0167
- ⊘ Pale pastel green 0240
- ⊠ Pale pastel pink 0336

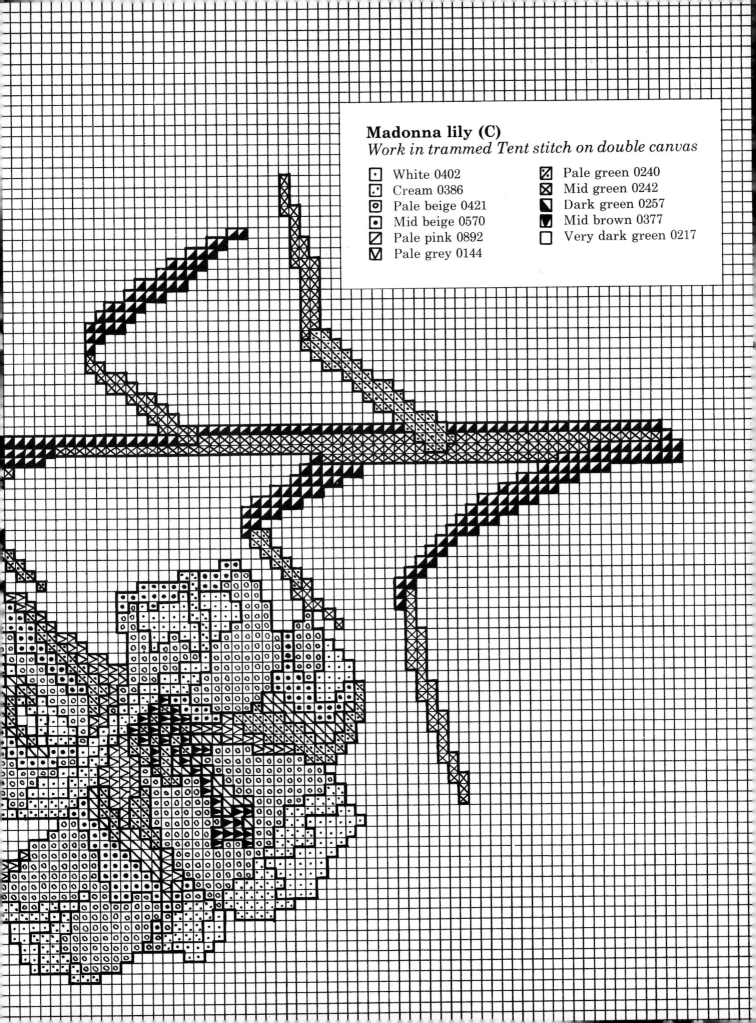

Madonna lily (C)
Work in trammed Tent stitch on double canvas

- ⊡ White 0402
- ⊡ Cream 0386
- ◉ Pale beige 0421
- ● Mid beige 0570
- ◪ Pale pink 0892
- ▽ Pale grey 0144
- ▨ Pale green 0240
- ⊠ Mid green 0242
- ◣ Dark green 0257
- ◥ Mid brown 0377
- ☐ Very dark green 0217

Back cover colour charts

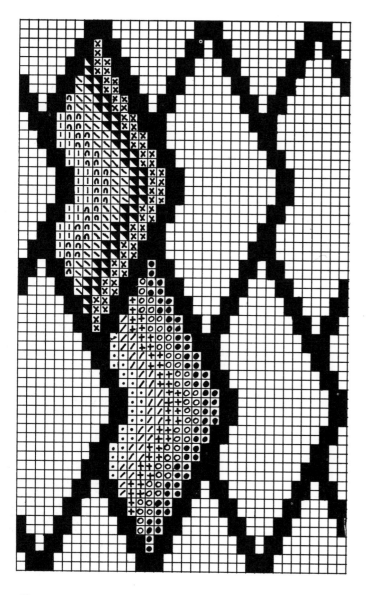

These charts for designs worked in Upright Gobelin stitch are shown in colour on the back cover. The designs can be made on any size canvas as long as the yarn chosen covers the canvas completely. Each sample can be made into a cushion and finished with a backing of velvet and silk cord around the seams

Left *Overlapping shell pattern in reds and greens repeating within black lines*
Opposite above *Chequered diamond pattern in blues and browns. Heavy black lines indicate positions of repeats which include part of white border*
Below *Double diamonds in red and white showing repeat groups within worked geometric borders*

Left
- ■ Black 0403
- ⊠ Dark red 045
- ◣ Red 019
- ◩ Light red 013
- ⌂ Pink 037
- ⊙ Dark green 0246
- ◉ Green 0245
- + Mid green 0243
- ◪ Light green 0242
- · Cream 0386
- ⊡ White 0402

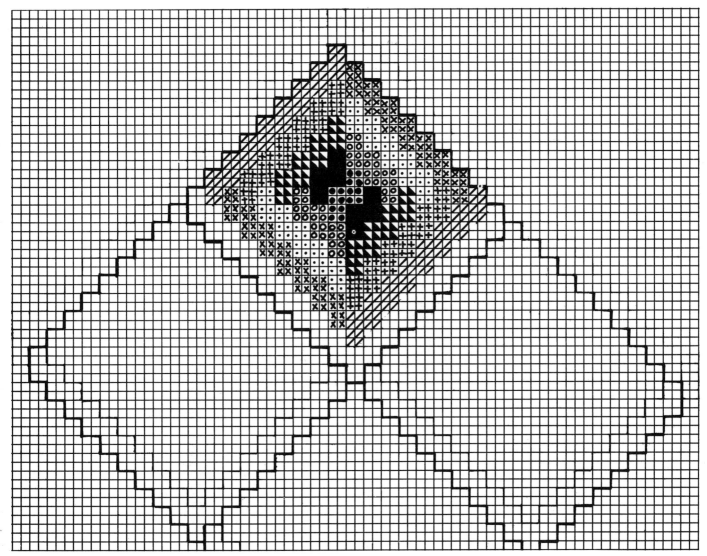

Above

☐ White 0402
⊙ Navy 0850
◎ Blue 0145
· Light blue 0160
⊠ Grey 0144
■ Dark brown 0360
◪ Tan 0258
⊞ Gold 0309
⊘ Beige 0388

Right

■ Dark red 045
⊙ Red 0412
⊠ Deep pink 010
◎ Pale pink 09
⊘ Dark grey 0400
⊞ Light grey 0497
· Cream 0386
▯ White 0402

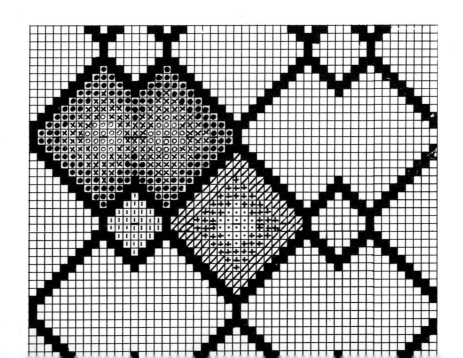

Borders and frames

Border design

Working design shows half the chart, work a mirror image to complete. Use trammed Tent stitch on double canvas. There are twenty-one different colours

Background
- ◉ Sky – pale pink 023
- ⊡ Clouds – white 0402

Birds
- ■ Black 0403
- ⊡ White 0402
- ▼ Dark brown 0986
- ⊠ Mid brown 0984
- ⊿ Red 0412
- ⊿ Blue 0133

Border background
- ◣ Mid green 0216
- ◤ Dark green 0217

Violets
- ◩ Light violet 0118
- ◭ Dark violet 0123
- ⊡ White 0402
- ⊡ Pale green 0242
- ⊿ Mid green 0257

Snowdrops
- ⊡ White 0402
- ◉ Cream 0421

Primroses
- ⊡ Pale green 0242
- ⊠ Mid green 0257
- ◉ Cream 0421
- ⊘ Pale yellow 0305
- ⊠ Dark yellow 0308
- ⊠ Mid green 0257
- ⊡ Pale green 0242

Morning Glory
- ⊘ Pale blue 0564
- ▼ Mid blue 0168
- ⊡ White 0402
- ⊠ Mid yellow 0308
- ⊿ Mid green 0257
- ⊡ Pale green 0242

Daisies
- ⊡ White 0402
- ◉ Cream 0421
- ⊘ Mid yellow 0306
- ⊠ Dark yellow 0308
- ⊡ Pale green 0242

A design often needs to be finished off with a border of stitching before it is placed in its position on a chair, framed on a wall or used as a cushion. Many ideas for such borders can come from embroidered ribbons, tartans, floor tiling or just plain checks and stripes. For example, if the design is a sampler cushion make a small ribbon motif of fleur-de-lys in one colour set into a background of another colour both of which harmonize with the central design. One can also use a sharp contrast that will immediately draw the eye towards the centre, such as black and white checks to border a formal flower design. Tiny waves of Florentine stitch could be used to surround huge waves of Florentine stitch. Sometimes the border can become part of the actual design or picture as illustrated in the design shown, where the flower border is part of the picture.

The same ideas apply when actually framing pictures of needlepoint tapestries. These frames can be stitched and then mounted onto the wooden frame intended for the design. The ideas for such frames are exactly the same as the borders but could be carried a little further.

For example, if one were doing a design of a farmyard scene, one of the pigs in the scene could actually run across the frame, itself stitched in the same manner as the background of the picture. Needlepoint tapestry frames mounted onto wooden frames can be used alone as surrounds for a portrait, photographs, drawings, etc. When the frames are used in this way they can be made to correspond with what they contain. As an example, if the frame is used for a photograph of a person, the needlepoint design can pick out little motifs of that person's life; flowers, cars, sailing boats, foxes, stripes of school or club colours etc can be used.

Backgrounds

In most needlepoint tapestry designs the background takes up a large proportion of the work. This can become tedious to do and very often the work drifts on for years without being finished because of the dullness of doing Tent stitch background in a neutral or dark colour. There are many ways of overcoming this and in addition greatly enhancing the finished design. For example, if the background does need to be in simple Tent stitch in a pale colour, it is very effective to work in tones of that colour so that the finished result looks 'old' and slightly streaky in the same way as Oriental carpets. Another method is to use very subtle stripes of Florentine stitch, sometimes using a strand of crewel wool with the tapestry wool to enhance a particular colour effect. If the background is a sky, then mother-of-pearl colours could be used to make it look like a dawn sky, or deepening blues like evening, or even a midnight sky of navy blue with white stars.

The background can also be used to great effect by making it textured with various different stitches being used together.

Marvellous brocaded and watered silk results can be achieved with clever use of stitches. Again the background can be turned into a sky with clouds in different stitches or it could become a sea of stitched waves. There are hundreds of things which can be done with backgrounds to make them not only interesting to work but also beautiful to see.

The design at right shows a black and white dog against a white garden fence. The fence is the background and the dog blends into it thus making the background a vital part of the design. This illustrates the need to make every part of the stitching important to the finished result.

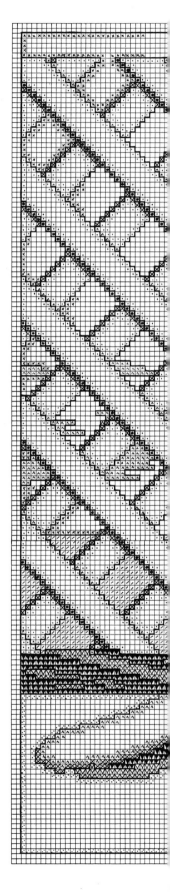

Dalmatian and white fence background
Work in trammed Tent stitch on double canvas. There are fifteen colours

Grass
- ⊡ Pale green 0242
- ⩔ Mid green 0257
- ⩗ Dark green 0243
- ◺ Very dark green 0218

Dog
- ⬟ Cream 0386
- ⊙ Pink 067
- ⊕ Pale grey 0144
- ⊠ Mid grey 0431
- ⬛ Dark grey 0398
- ■ Black 0403

Sky
- ⊠ Blue 0564
- ⌂ Cream 0386

Trees
- ⊘ Pale green 0215
- ⊠ Mid green 0216

Landscape
- ⊘ Light brown/green 0842

Fence
- ⊡ White 0402
- ⬜ Cream 0386
- ⊠ Mid grey 0431
- ⊙ Very dark grey 0401

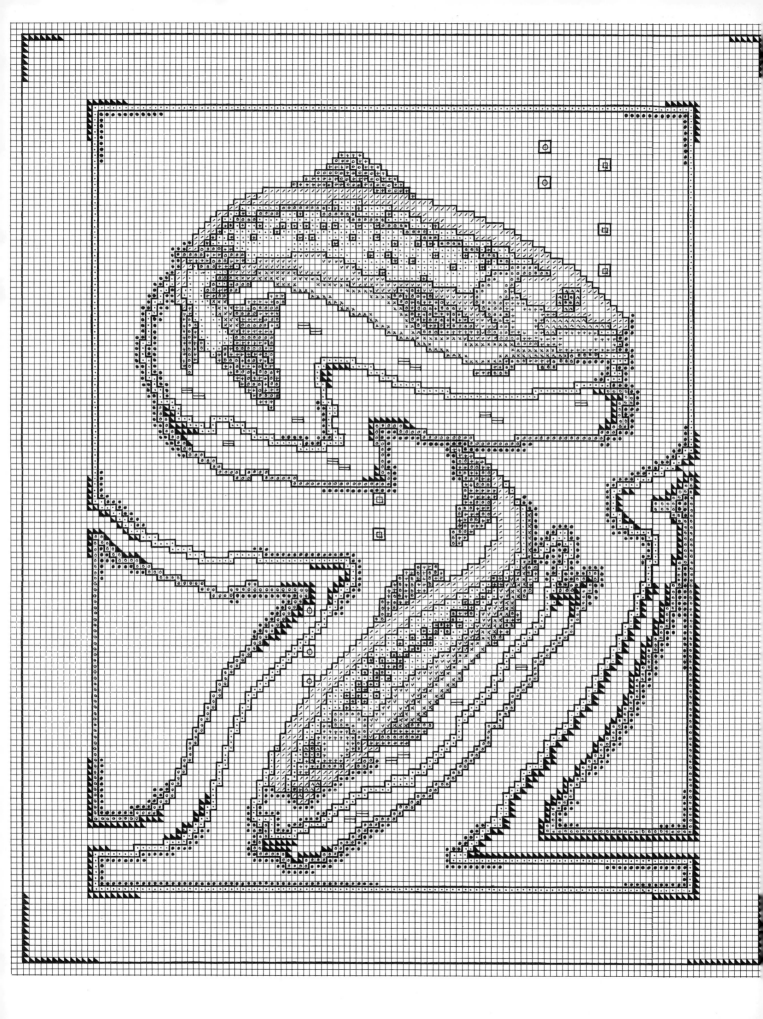

Silver, gold, beads and sequins

Silver and gold work, like beadwork, is really a separate book, however, it can be used in needlepoint tapestry as highlights or to achieve a specific result. For instance, a seed pearl threaded through and placed in position where a tent stitch would have been will make a more intense spot of light than a stitch in white wool. Likewise a sequin can be threaded through in the same way to give a twinkle. Equally gold or silver threads can be used alone, as long as they cover the canvas, or in conjunction with crewel wool or tapestry wool, in order to get the required shine. For instance, if a crown of gold is in the design then it could be of gold thread. Similarly a dog could have a gold collar. Obviously, if the design is going to be used a great deal and will need cleaning then care must be taken before embarking on seed pearls, sequins or golden threads for these are difficult to clean and may have to be re-stitched afterwards. The working design shows a silver fish in sparkling water blowing bubbles of sequins.

Fish

Work on single canvas 20 holes to 1 inch in Petit Point Tent stitch using Clark's Anchor stranded cotton and silver and gold thread. Finish with sequins and silver beads where indicated

- Silver thread
- Gold thread
- Dark green 0212
- Dark blue 0139
- Pale aquamarine 0185
- Pale green 0203
- Pale pink 099
- Pale blue 0160
- Pale russet/gold 0366
- Silver sequins
- Gold sequins
- Silver beads

Alphabets

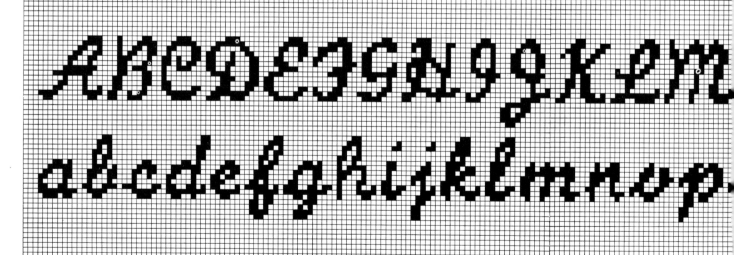

A, B

The following designs for alphabets are easy and extremely interesting to work. First of all a sampler can be designed using any one of these three. Later a whole poem could be worked. Alphabets can be stitched all in the same colour or each letter can be a different colour; they may be striped like bull's eyes or chequered like a draught board. They can be made enormous or tiny depending on the design.

C

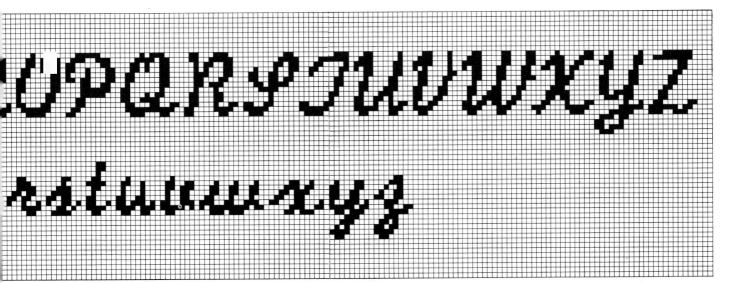

OPQRSTUVWXYZ
RSTUVWXYZ

Working design A. This classical serifed alphabet can be made into a more ornate design by extending the strokes on the ends which are known as serifs. These can be incorporated into a motif or design so that the words become an integral part of the pattern.

Working design B. A plain and very simple alphabet whose letters can be condensed or extended to fit the character and mood of the design.

Working design C. This specially designed script can be used to write a whole needle-point tapestry letter to someone, to sign a name, to wish someone Happy Birthday or merely as a sampler.

Work on any size canvas, in any colour, in trammed Tent or Cross stitch, or incorporate into your own design

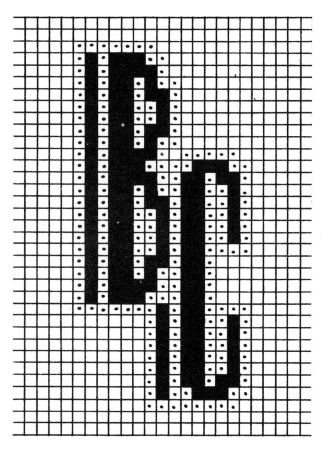

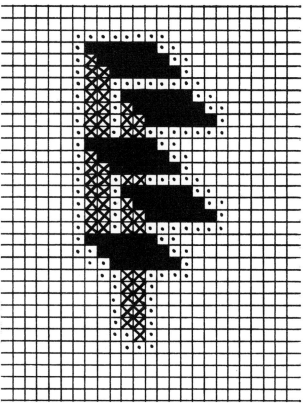

Monograms and words

Designs on the left show how to intertwine letters together to form a monogram. BC and EF have been selected as one contains curves and the other straight lines. Monograms can be worked on a piece of canvas and later turned into a purse, bag, pocket, cushion, etc. They are really the simplest form of personal design and a monogrammed present is almost always accepted with pleasure.

Lettering can be worked in such a way as to become three dimensional by using tones of a colour. It can also make word games by punning on the letter. For example, the letter B can be striped like a bee or even have tiny little bees inside the shape of the B. The letter C can be made to look like the sea and so on.

The design on the right shows how to work a word and elaborate it at the same time. The word is ROSE so the theme becomes roses. All flowers could be worked in this way. In fact, once the ideas begin there is no end to the words which can be played upon.

Monograms BC EF
Work in Tent stitch on any canvas in any colour combinations, and use appropriate yarns
Rose
Work in trammed Tent stitch on double canvas

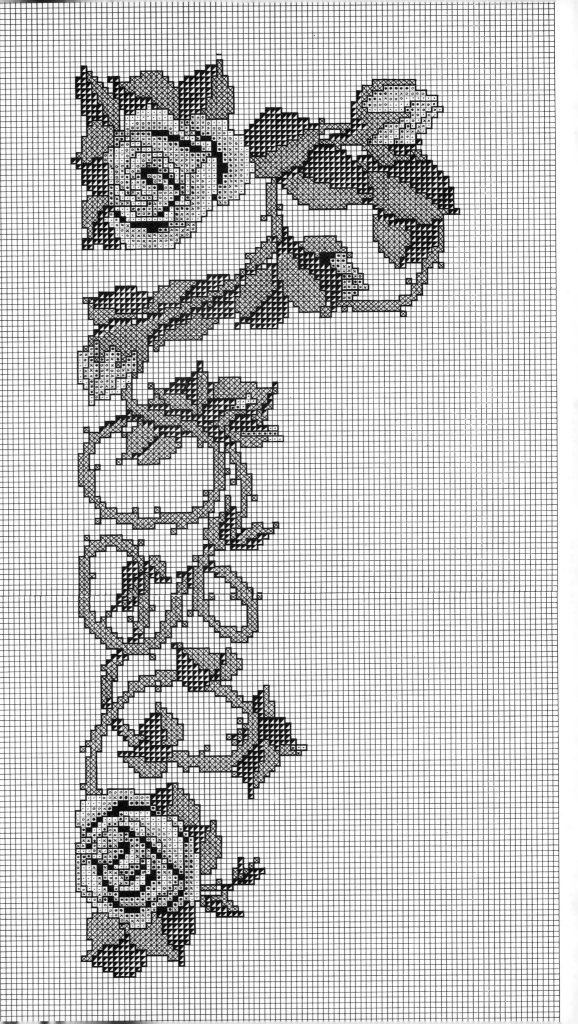

	Pale pink 0336
	Light pink 09
	Mid pink 010
	Dark pink 013
	Very dark pink 019
	Mid green 0243
	Dark green 0245

Background

Deep brown 0360

Chairs and stools

There are a great variety of chairs and stools which are traditionally covered in needle-point tapestry. These drawings illustrate various designs of eighteenth and nineteenth century chairs which were traditionally in tapestry. Most good needlework shops sell the traditional designs; however it is some-times interesting to break with tradition and make up an entirely new design. See also deck chair page 70.

Design for a William and Mary chair with one huge flower instead of the traditional circle or garland of flowers.

Working design (repeating detail), opposite, for a dining chair in Florentine stitch which is broken here and there with checks.

Each of these designs must have patterns cut by experienced upholsterers to ensure that the finished tapestry will fit the chair.

Work in trammed Tent stitch on 10 holes to 1 inch double canvas. Extend the background to suit the size of your chair

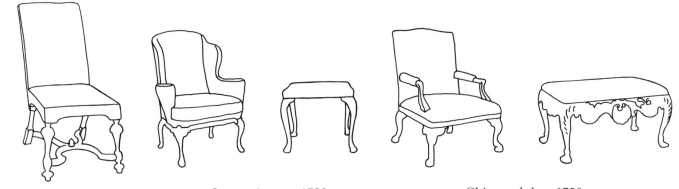

William and Mary c 1690   *Queen Anne c 1720*   *Chippendale c 1750*

Flower design

Tulip

- ☐ Pale pink 023
- ◩ Mid pink 067
- ▨ Deep pink 068
- ■ Very dark pink 071

Leaves

- ▨ Light green 0216
- ■ Dark green 0217

Background

- ▨ Pale ice green 0265
- ▨ Pale sludge green 0842

Chequered design

- ■ Black 0403
- ⊠ Deep red 019
- ⊙ Deep green 0246

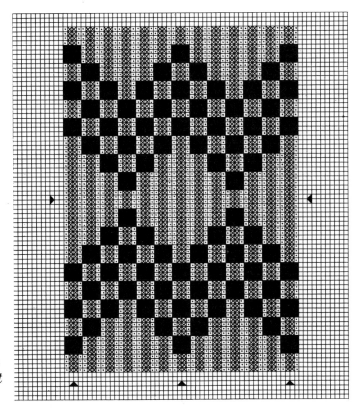

Work in Chequer stitch and plain Tent stitch on single canvas 18 holes to one inch. Repeat the design to suit the size of your chair

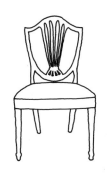
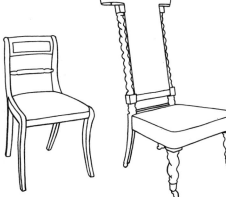

Chippendale
c 1750   *Robert Adam*
c 1770   *Sheraton c 1795*   *Regency c 1810*   *Victorian c 1845*   *Stool c 1850*

Front cover jacket

Work in trammed Tent stitch on 10 holes to 1 inch double canvas. Fronts and Sleeves are mirror images. The jacket is to fit sizes 34 inch to 36 inch. Stretch and trim canvas to within 1 inch of work. With right sides together back-stitch with blue tapestry wool along edge of work, press seams open with a damp cloth. Start with sleeve seams, then stitch the fronts to the back in the usual way. Press seams as you work. Cut out lining from a paper pattern made from finished work with the usual $\frac{5}{8}$ inch seam allowances. Make the lining in the same way as the jacket, using a medium weight interlining in both fronts. Set in jacket sleeves making sure that rainbow stripes match on shoulders and sleeves. Insert and catch stitch purchased shoulder pads between jacket and lining. Hand or machine stitch lining into jacket. Press work with a damp cloth.

Clouds
- Light salmon 067
- Dark salmon 068

Sky
- Blue 0508

Seagull
- Light grey 0144
- Mid grey 0431
- Dark grey 0848

Sea
- Light green 0215
- Mid green 0216
- Dark green 0217

Rainbow
- Pale violet 095
- Very pale blue/grey 0431
- Very pale blue/green 0167
- Very pale cream 0570
- Very pale orange 0336
- Very pale red 067

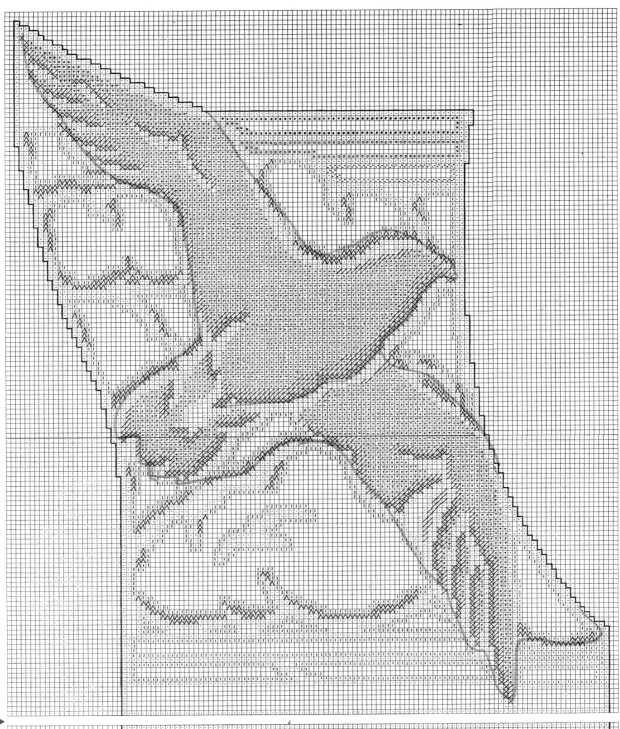

2 inches ▶

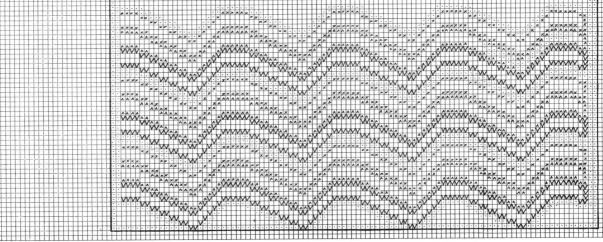

Front cover jacket

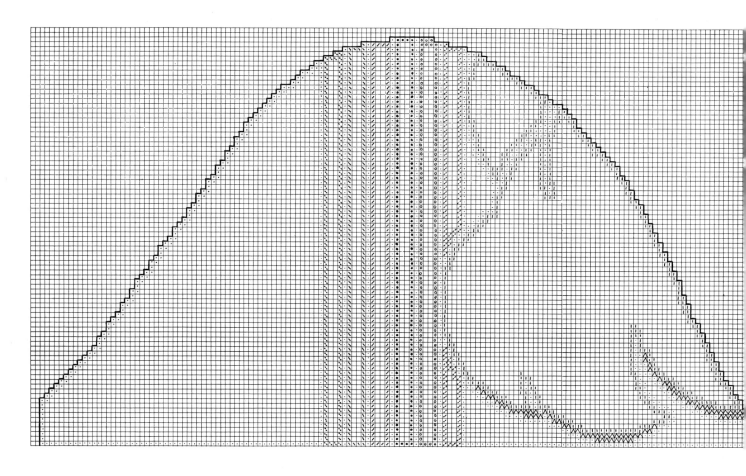

Sleeve

$7\frac{1}{2}$ inch

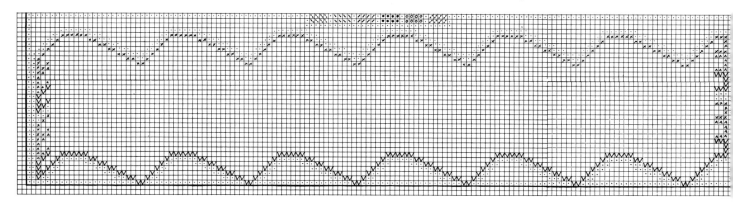

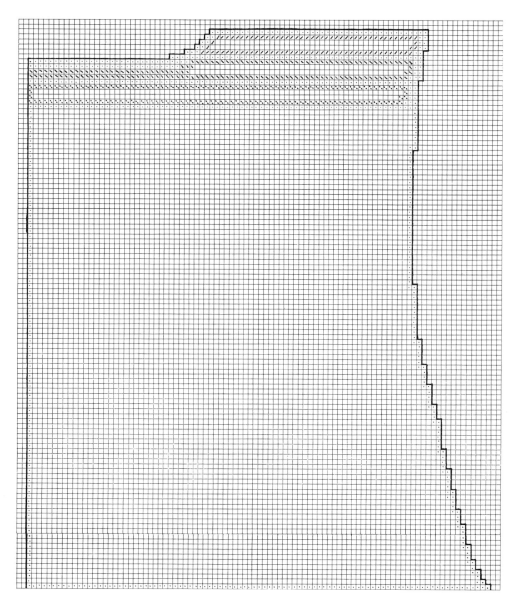

Clouds
- ⊡ Light salmon 067
- ◿ Dark salmon 068

Sky
- ⊡ Blue 0508

Seagull
- ⊞ Light grey 0144
- ◿ Mid grey 0431
- ⊠ Dark grey 0848

Sea
- ⊠ Light green 0215
- ⋀ Mid green 0216
- ⋁ Dark green 0217

Rainbow
- ⊡ Pale violet 095
- ⊙ Very pale blue/grey 0431
- ⊙ Very pale blue/green 0167
- ◿ Very pale cream 0570
- ◹ Very pale orange 0336
- ⊡ Very pale red 067

$3\frac{1}{2}$ inch

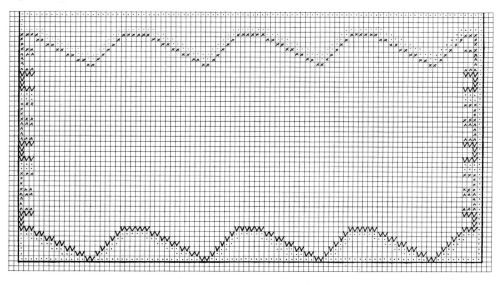

Back

Rainbow and evening bags

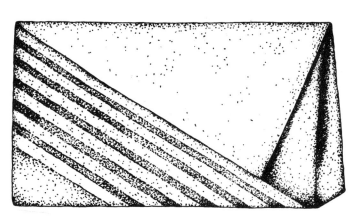

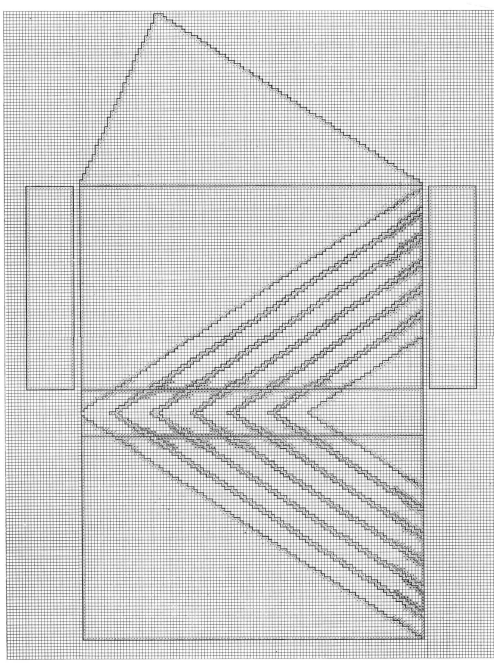

Rainbow bag

- ⊡ Sky blue 0508
- ⊡ Rainbow – pale violet 095
- ⊙ Pale blue/grey 0431
- ⊙ Pale blue/green 0167
- ⊿ Pale cream 0570
- ⊠ Pale orange 0336
- ⊡ Pale red 067

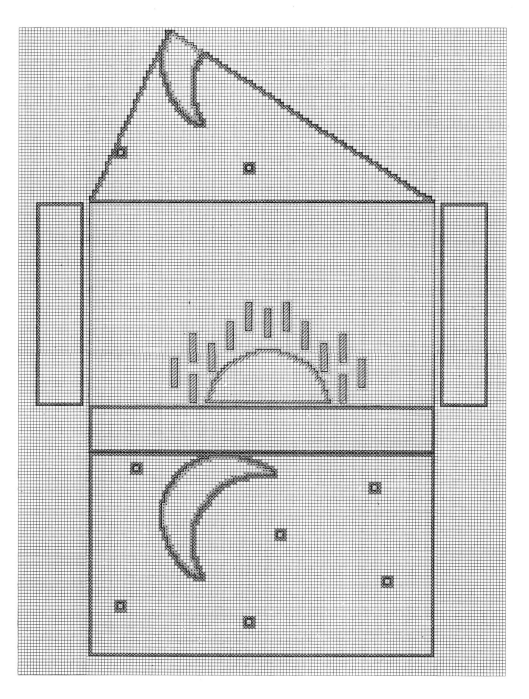

Evening bag

⊠ Dark blue 0148
⊕ Stars – silver sequins
⊡ Moon – silver thread;
use enough strands to
cover the canvas com-
pletely, or Petit Point
⊡ Pale blue 0158
⊘ Sun – gold thread; use
enough strands to cover
the canvas completely

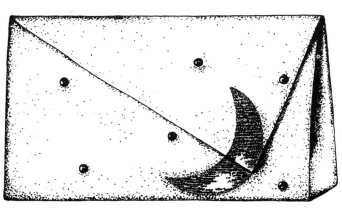

*Work in trammed Tent stitch on 10 holes to
1 inch double canvas. Trim to within 1 inch of
work. To make up, back stitch front and back
to side gussets. Line with light weight canvas*

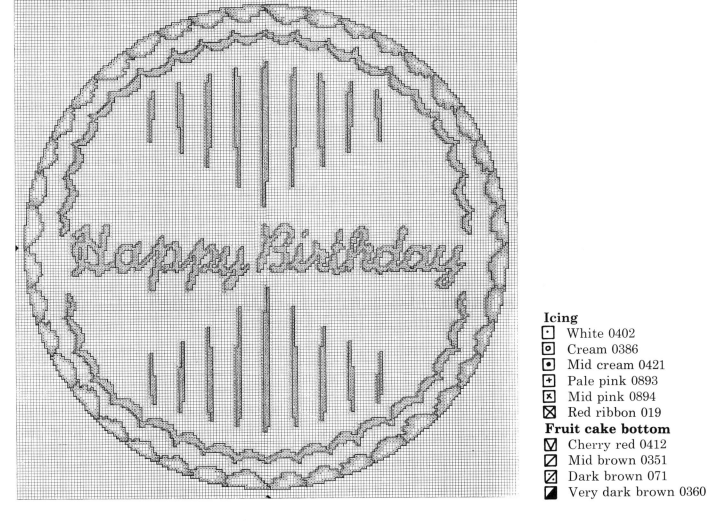

Icing

⊡	White	0402
⊙	Cream	0386
⊙	Mid cream	0421
⊞	Pale pink	0893
⊠	Mid pink	0894
⊠	Red ribbon	019

Fruit cake bottom

▽	Cherry red	0412
◩	Mid brown	0351
◩	Dark brown	071
◪	Very dark brown	0360

Cushions

Cake cushion
Work in trammed Tent stitch on 10 holes to 1 inch double canvas. To make up, trim work, stitch with right sides together, leaving enough of the back seam open to get the filling in

Charlie Chaplin cushion
Work in trammed Tent stitch on 10 holes to 1 inch double canvas

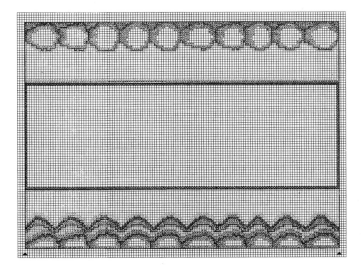

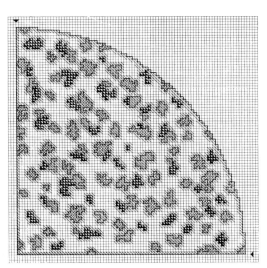

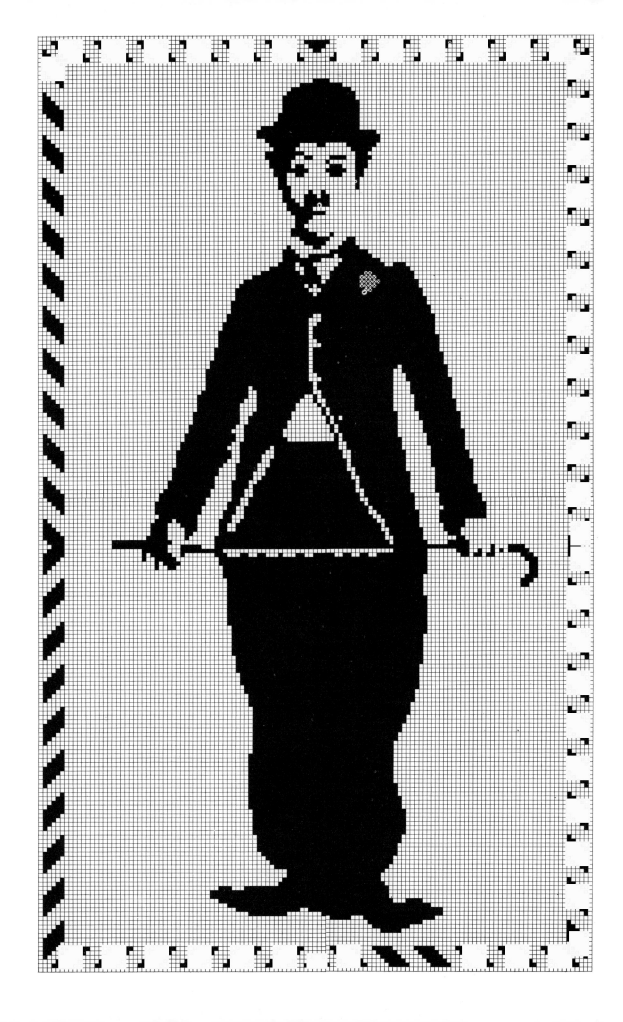

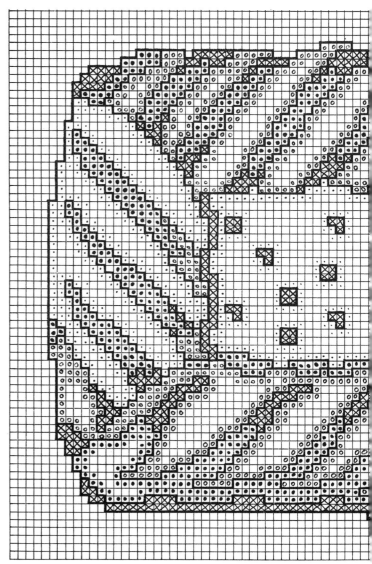

Trompe l'oeil

This working design takes the deck chair right out of the ordinary, serviceable garden chair bracket and makes it into a marvellous sitting-room chair. Lots of designs can be worked out for a deck chair as long as you cut the pattern from the actual size of the chair and allow 2 inches all around.

Deck chair

Work in Cross stitch on 10 holes to 3 inches rug canvas with Paton's Turkey rug wool. To make up, trim, and line with medium weight canvas

- [·] Beige 939
- [⊙] Mastic 940
- [●] Light tan 863
- [⊠] Dark tan 941
- [ ] Loam brown 903

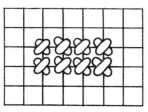

Recommended Cross stitch variation to be worked on coarse canvas

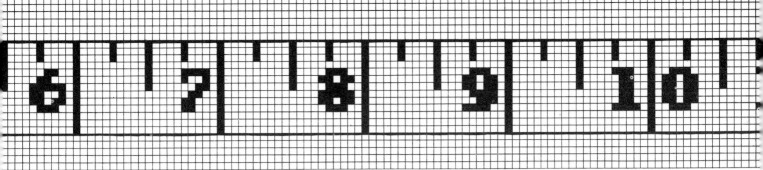

Tape measure belt

Work in trammed Tent stitch on 10 holes to 1 inch double canvas, or in Petit Point on 20 holes to 1 inch single canvas to reflect the actual waist measurement. To make up, trim work, turn seams and press. Line with light weight canvas, and attach clasp

☐ Yellow 0311   ◼ Black 0403

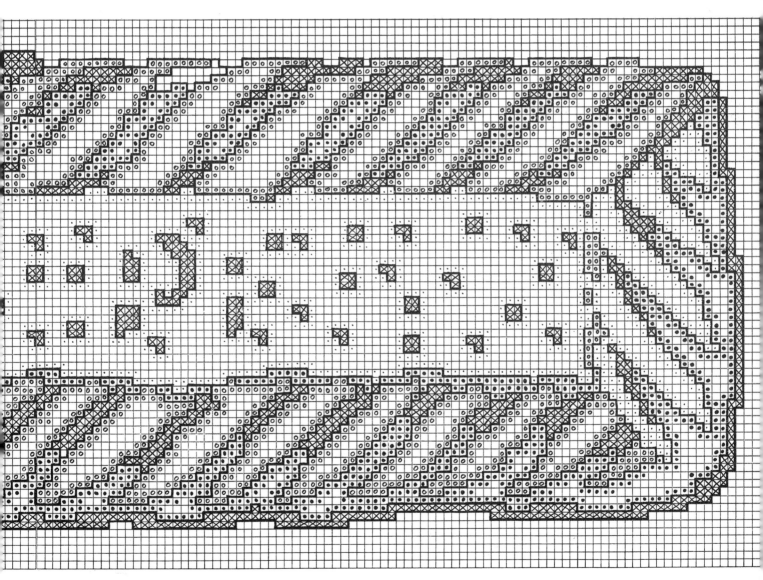

Eastern carpet

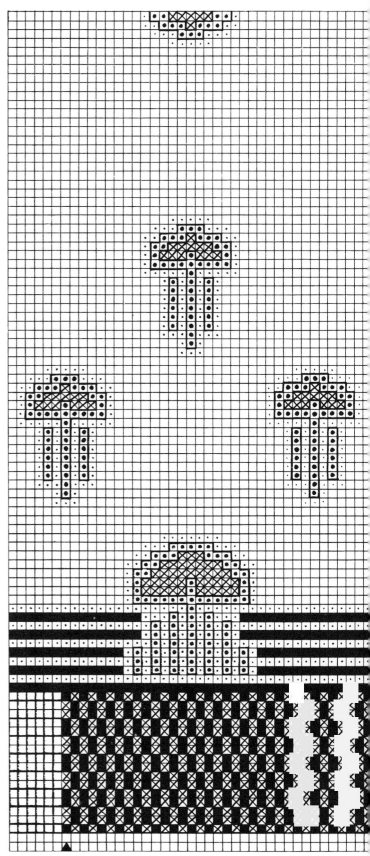

Work in Cross stitch on 10 holes to 3 inches rug canvas. Use Patons Turkey rug wool. To make up, turn edges, stitch and tape. The chart shows one quarter of the finished carpet. Complete design by working mirror images. Cross stitch variation see page 70

■ Black 52   · Poker red 909
⊙ Blue haze 896   ⊠ Dark rust 911

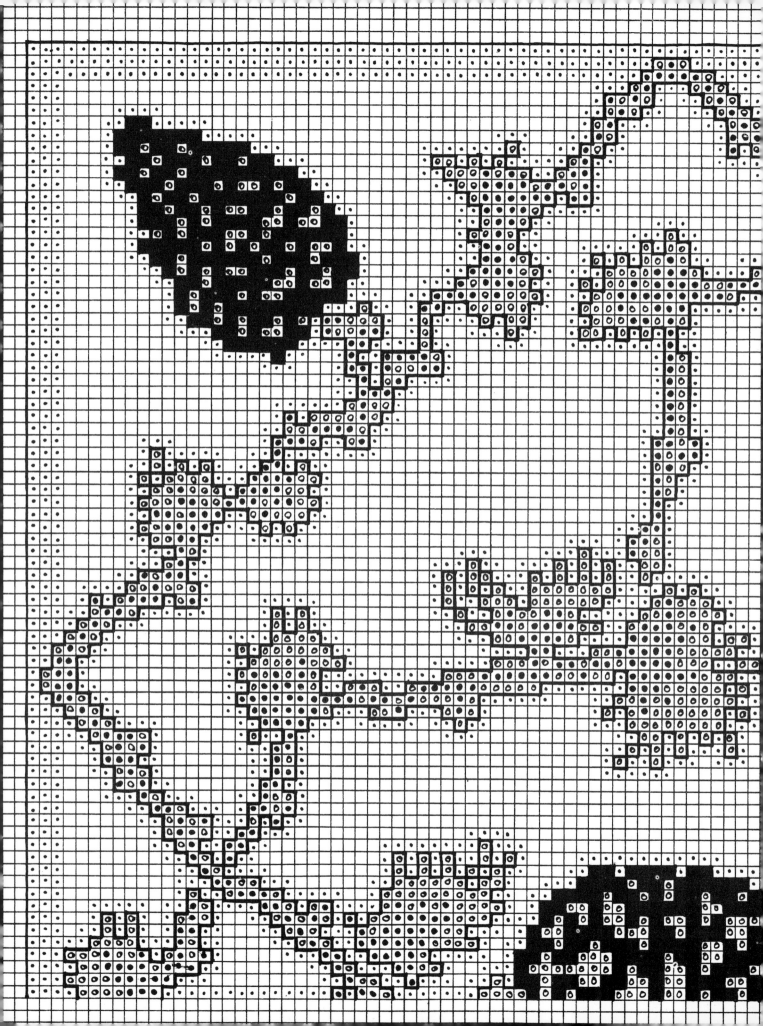

Tufted carpet

Work in Velvet stitch on 10 holes to 3 inches rug canvas. Use Patons Turkey rug wool. Repeat the fir cone design as many times as you like to make whatever size of carpet desired. To finish, cut Velvet stitch loops, turn in edges, stitch and back with canvas.

- ⊡ Light biscuit 973
- ⊙ Mastic 940
- ⊚ Dark tan 941
- ■ Loam brown 903

Portrait
of a house

Sky
☒ Light blue 0158

Grass
⊡ Mid green 0242
Ⅴ Dark green 0257

Trees and shrubs
☒ Very dark green 0217
◉ Green/black 0218
▼ Mid pink 068

Roof
◪ Concrete buff 0376
◿ Very pale warm brown 0388
◺ Pale warm brown 0373
◹ Mid warm brown 0418
◸ Dark warm brown 0419
▯ Mid cool brown 0984
◪ Brick red 0349
◿ Dark brick red 0350

Front
⊡ White 0402
◉ Grey 0144
◪ Brick red 0349
◿ Dark brick red 0350
⊞ Shutters – blue 0161
■ Black 0403

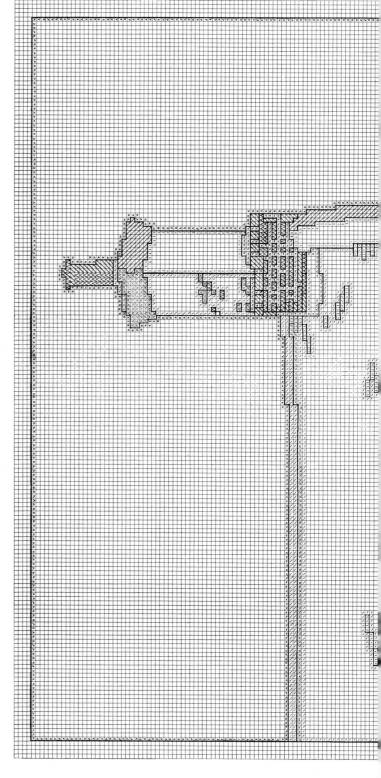

Work in trammed Tent stitch on 10 holes to 1 inch double canvas

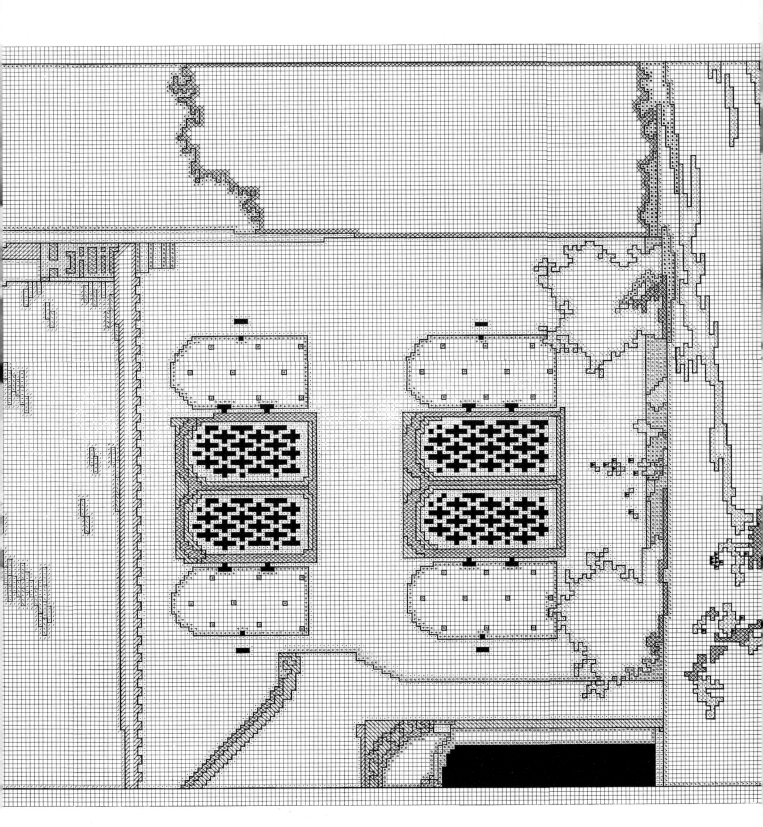

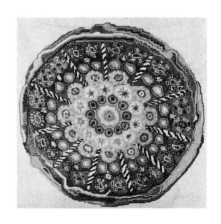

How to make your own designs

Although it is interesting and absorbing to work needlepoint tapestry from existing designs it sometimes happens that you cannot find the exact design required for a particular room, chair etc, in which case the only thing to do is make your own design. This is infinitely more rewarding because you will have created a piece of work from start to finish. Making one's own designs is not really difficult and there are a variety of methods:

1. If you are unable to draw, trace a flower, photograph or magazine cutting of the type of thing you want. Use a graph tracing paper if you can; there are various sizes of metric and imperial made by Chartwell and generally available through stationers. If you have to use ordinary tracing paper, pin the tracing made to graph paper, so that the squares on the graph will correspond to the squares of the canvas which is going to be used. Then, having selected the colours you want to use, give each colour a symbol, such as shown in this book, and mark the symbols on the tracing paper so that there is a symbol for each square of the graph paper underneath, or in each square of the tracing graph paper. NB The size of the finished design will depend on the grade of canvas being used.

2. If you can draw, make a simple line drawing design directly onto graph paper and make colour symbols in each square.

Above *Mille fleurs glass paperweight worked into needlepoint design for a cushion by Kaffe Fassett, shown on back cover*
Left *The famous Andy Warhol Campbell's soup tin goes a stage further made life size for a door stop or giant size as a stool*

See end papers for these designs in colour

3. If you want to use more than one figure or motif in a design use either of the above methods. In a repeating design use a mirror to mirror the original motif so that you can judge how it will look in duplicate.

4. If the design is going to be very big, for example a carpet, then it is advisable to put the complete design down in miniature on graph paper so that you can see how it will look. Then take a large scale graph paper and work out a repeating detail so that this particular graph can be the working design whereas the small one will be a guide to the finished work. When plotting a design it is best to start from middle of work and then move outwards or from the four sides and work inwards.

5. When working with abstract colour designs such as Florentine work, it is best to work out the colour sequence on a separate piece of canvas. Then, work a triangular section of waves from each of the four sides to meet in the middle. Make the first shape of the wave and then fill in with the correct colour sequence. The centre of the design will just happen. This particular way of working will give you a centre to the work; however, if you wish the Florentine shapes to move up the canvas then just draw a wavy line in India ink and work this line in the

Left   Mirror image butterfly and flower carpet designed by Kaffe Fassett. The carpet is made in many different stitches which heighten the overall effect of butterflies fluttering over flowers

Right   Valentino's cushions take needlepoint into shell shapes and colours. Great and small shells of various types worked the whole way round in needlepoint or, for the flat scallops backed in tweed or velvet of a suitable colour

first of the colour sequence and then continue according to colour.

6. When doing needlepoint tapestry for chairs, upholstery or slippers it is important to ask an upholsterer or shoemaker to make a pattern for you. From this pattern of chair, or the upper of a slipper in the correct size, you can cut your canvas shape, allowing 2 inches all around the work, and then plot your pattern. This is *extremely* important. Nothing would be more annoying than to design and make a whole chair cover or pair of slippers and then find that the cover will not fit the chair nor the upper the foot.

7. When the work for either upholstery or footwear is finished it should be sent to the appropriate upholsterer or cobbler to make up and complete.

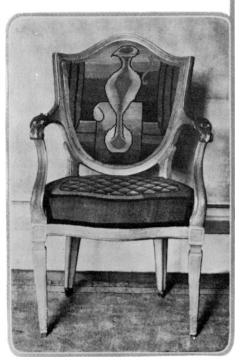

1920's

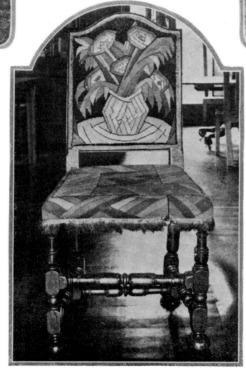

Above *Three designs by Duncan Grant, the one on the far right has been worked by Vanessa Bell. Shown in Vogue in 1923.*

Below *A design by Roger Fry, worked by Winifred Gill. Note the way two of the designs are continued down the front of the seat.*